MODERN
SPIRITUAL
MASTERS

Also by Robert Ellsberg

All Saints: Daily Reflections on
Saints, Prophets, and Witnesses for Our Time

The Saints' Guide to Happiness

Blessed Among All Women

As Editor:

The Duty of Delight: The Diaries of Dorothy Day

Dorothy Day: Selected Writings

Gandhi on Christianity

Fritz Eichenberg: Works of Mercy

Charles de Foucauld: Essential Writings

Flannery O'Connor: Spiritual Writings

Carlo Carretto: Essential Writings

Thich Nhat Hanh: Essential Writings

MODERN SPIRITUAL MASTERS

Writings on Contemplation and Compassion

EDITED BY
ROBERT ELLSBERG

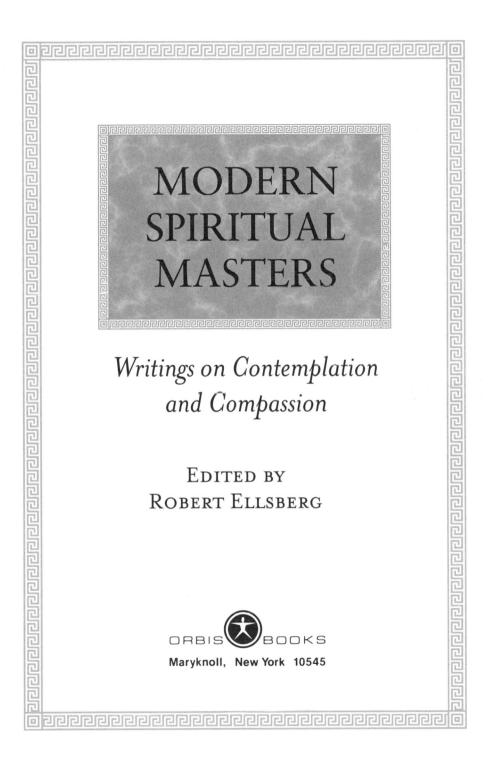

ORBIS BOOKS

Maryknoll, New York 10545

Founded in 1970, Orbis Books endeavors to publish works that enlighten the mind, nourish the spirit, and challenge the conscience. The publishing arm of the Maryknoll Fathers and Brothers, Orbis seeks to explore the global dimensions of the Christian faith and mission, to invite dialogue with diverse cultures and religious traditions, and to serve the cause of reconciliation and peace. The books published reflect the views of their authors and do not represent the official position of the Maryknoll Society. To learn more about Maryknoll and Orbis Books, please visit our website at www.maryknoll.org.

Library of Congress Cataloging-in-Publication Data

Modern spiritual masters : writings on contemplation and compassion / edited by Robert Ellsberg.
     p. cm. – (Modern spiritual masters)
   ISBN 978-1-57075-788-4
   1. Spiritual life. 2. Contemplation. 3. Compassion – Religious aspects. 4. Spiritual life – Christianity. 5. Compassion – Religious aspects – Christianity. I. Ellsberg, Robert, 1955-
BL624.M632 2008
204 – dc22

                                2008019681

Contents

Introduction

From time immemorial, those seeking to learn or grow in the spiritual life have apprenticed themselves to authoritative guides, or spiritual masters. Such guides have gone by different names, whether guru, staretz, abbot, or Mother. The disciples who followed Jesus addressed him initially as "Rabbi (which means Teacher)." What such teachers have shared in common was that they embodied the content of their teaching. Having attained some considerable degree of wisdom or enlightenment, they were able to convey those qualities to others — not just by words, but by their way of life. Those who followed them learned not just by studying their discourse on spiritual topics, but by living with them, observing how they prayed, how they worked, how they responded to ethical challenges.

That is how it was for the original disciples of Jesus; they entered into his teaching by literally following him about. "What are you seeking?" he asked some of them, former disciples of John the Baptist, who were tagging along after him. "Where do you live?" they asked, to which he replied with a simple invitation: "Come and see."

The "modern spiritual masters" in this volume are all successors to those disciples. Like the original seekers whom Jesus called, they accepted his invitation to "come and see," to spend their lives in his company, to see the world through his eyes, to judge things according to his values. And so, in turn, through their writings and actions, they came to serve as guides for many others.

The twelve men and women whose writings are included here do not represent the full spectrum of Christian discipleship, though they embraced a variety of paths. They were nuns, monks, priests, bishops, and lay people. They could be described as mystics, prophets, and social activists. One of them, Mohandas Gandhi, was a Hindu, who nevertheless sought to apply the principles of the Sermon on the Mount to the struggle for peace and freedom. Mother Maria Skobtsova, an Orthodox nun, sought to pioneer a form of monasticism in the world, and died as a martyr in a Nazi death camp. Oscar Romero, the prophetic archbishop of San Salvador, was shot while saying Mass. Mother Teresa of Calcutta

1

sought to recognize the face of Christ among the poorest of the poor. Henri Nouwen, a charismatic priest and spiritual writer, found his true home among a community of mentally disabled adults and their helpers.

What did they have in common? In different ways they showed the importance of integrating a contemplative life with a compassionate response to the needs of the world. In part because of their influence, this perspective may not seem remarkable. And yet it has been common through much of Christian history to draw a distinction between these options: the *via contemplativa* and the *via apostolica*. Sometimes these ways were personified in terms of the disciples Mary and Martha, devoted friends of Jesus. While Martha, busy in the kitchen, worried about "many things," her sister Mary (the "contemplative," sitting at Jesus' feet), was said to have chosen "the better part."

Many Christians, it is true, have opposed this artificial distinction. St. Francis of Assisi, for example, saw no conflict between mystical prayer and his service among the poor. St. Ignatius Loyola, founder of the Society of Jesus, charged his Jesuits to be "contemplatives in action." Most of the figures assembled here reached back farther still to the example and message of Jesus, who obviously combined a prayerful life with compassion for the poor, sick, and marginalized of his time. He asserted a radical equivalence between the love of God and the love of neighbor. By his own identification with the poor, Jesus went so far as to warn that our salvation rests on how we respond to the "least" of our brothers and sisters.

This should be plain enough. And yet Christians throughout the ages have often found it hard to maintain this balance. The temptation to identify the gospel with sound doctrine, codes of behavior, liturgical rubrics, and ritual purity, has been so strong that it requires the occasional jolt of a Mother Maria Skobtsova to remind us, "At the Last Judgment I shall not be asked whether I was successful in my ascetic exercises, nor how many bows and prostrations I made. Instead I shall be asked, Did I feed the hungry, clothe the naked, visit the sick and the prisoners?"

These modern spiritual masters strongly opposed a style of spirituality focused solely on the interior life and disengaged from the needs and struggles of the world. Their similarity on this point amounts to a kind of family resemblance, despite the differences in their theology or the specific forms of their vocation. Some, like Mother Teresa and Catherine de Hueck Doherty, expressed their devotion to Christ through direct and personal service of the poor. For Madeleine Delbrêl, it was a matter of bearing witness to Christ through the duties and demands of ordinary life among her working-class neighbors. For Dom Helder Camara and Oscar Romero, authentic love for the poor involved challenging the structures of social injustice that gave rise to poverty. For Sister Thea Bowman it meant honoring the struggles of African Americans and celebrating their gifts to the church. Each in their different ways tried to discover what it means to love God with one's whole heart and to love one's neighbor as oneself.

And yet, despite their engagement with the world, it is important to emphasize that they did not simply become social workers or political activists. Their response was rooted in prayer, nurtured by attention to the interior life and the need for silence, solitude, and times of withdrawal. This solitude might entail, for Thomas Merton, the contemplative life of a Trappist monastery, or, for Madeleine Delbrêl, a moment of reflection in the midst of a crowded subway. Howard Thurman spoke of entering the "temple of quiet in one's own spirit," while Catherine de Hueck Doherty described the *poustinia* — a hut in the forest, a room in our house, or even a place in our hearts to which we can from time to time retreat. The contemplative life might mean different things, but for all these men and women it involved an intimacy with God that was at the same time also a window into the depths of their own history, allowing them to see what was important and true.

A spiritual master is ultimately a guide — someone who has traveled the path that lies before us. At the end of the day, such guides do not show us how to be like them, but how to be more truly ourselves, how to find our own hidden gifts, how to respond to the sacred voice that issues from our own hearts and from the challenges of our own time and place. The goal of the spiritual master is not that we should remain forever novices or apprentices, but that we should learn to walk our own path, and perhaps one day become a guide for others.

◆ ◆ ◆

This volume is a companion to the Modern Spiritual Masters Series that I have edited for Orbis Books. Nearly forty volumes have appeared in this series thus far, including most of the figures featured here. (In at least three cases, Mother Maria Skobtsova, Mother Teresa, and Howard Thurman, the Orbis volumes were the source of my selections.) This series, in turn, was partly inspired by my own book *All Saints: Daily*

Reflections on Saints, Prophets and Witnesses for Our Time (Crossroad, 1997), in which I offered 365 biographical meditations on holy and heroic people across the centuries. Almost all of the figures in the Modern Spiritual Masters Series were featured in *All Saints,* or in a companion volume, *Blessed Among All Women* (Crossroad, 2005). I am grateful to Crossroad for permitting me to adapt some of my own essays in those books for the biographical prefaces in this volume.

The immediate inspiration for this volume, however, came from Jack Jezreel and Joe Grant of JustFaith Ministries. This remarkable parish-based program has endeavored to inspire people of faith with a passion for social justice and a will to express that in active ministry. Thousands of people have passed through this rigorous program. And now Just-Faith intends to extend this initiative through a new program, "Engaging Spirituality," promoting a spiritual renewal that engages the needs of the world. As a resource for this program, Joe and Jack commissioned this volume and helped select the figures to include. I am grateful for their initiative and for all their encouragement. My years in publishing have taught me that every book is ultimately a team effort.

I am particularly grateful to my Orbis colleagues Doris Goodnough and Catherine Costello for their support and for their behind-the-scenes role in the publication of countless books that have "enlightened the mind, nourished the spirit, and challenged the conscience."

ONE

THOMAS MERTON

Contemplation and Compassion

In The Seven Storey Mountain, *the famous autobiography he wrote in his early years as a Trappist monk, Thomas Merton told a story — by turns funny and sad — of his search for his true identity and home, beginning with his orphaned childhood and his education in France, England, and eventually at Columbia University. He regarded himself as a true man of his age, free of any moral laws beyond his own making, ready to* "ransack and rob the world of all its pleasures and satisfactions." *But increasingly his life struck him more as a story of pride and selfishness that brought nothing but unhappiness to himself and others.* "What a strange thing!" *he wrote,* "In filling myself, I had emptied myself. In grasping things, I had lost everything. In devouring pleasures and joys, I had found distress and anguish and fear."

Out of this anguish and confusion, Merton found himself drawn by the sense that there must be a deeper end and purpose to existence. All around him the world was tumbling toward World War II, the ultimate achievement of "Contemporary Civilization." *Meanwhile he was reading Blake, St. Augustine, and medieval philosophy and beginning to suspect that* "the only way to live was in a world that was charged with the presence and reality of God."

It was a short leap from this insight to his reception in the Catholic church and ultimately to the Abbey of Gethsemani in Kentucky. The Trappists had captured his heart from the first time he read about them in The Catholic Encyclopedia. *When he later made a retreat at Gethsemani and there for the first time viewed the silent monks, dressed in their white habits and kneeling in prayer in the chapel, he felt that he had found his true home at last.* "This is the center of America," *he exclaimed.*

With the publication of Merton's autobiography, he was suddenly the most famous monk in America. The irony was not lost on him. He had become a Trappist in part to escape the claims of ego, the anxious desire to "be somebody." And yet his superiors felt his writing had something to offer the world and they ordered him to keep at it. And so he did. Yet for all the books he would go on to produce, in the public mind he was eternally fixed at the point where his memoir ended — as a young monk with his cowl pulled over his head, happily convinced that in joining an austere monastic community he had fled the modern world, never to return. It was difficult for readers to appreciate that this picture represented only the beginning of Merton's journey as a monk.

Over time he came to regret, in his youthful book, the attitude of pious scorn directed at "the world" and its unfortunate citizens. He had seemed to regard the monastery as a secluded haven set apart from "the news and desires and appetites and conflicts" that bedeviled ordinary humanity. Only with time did he realize that "the monastery is not an 'escape' from the world. On the contrary, by being in the monastery I take my true part in all the struggles and sufferings of the world." With this realization his writing assumed an increasingly compassionate and ecumenical tone.

In one of his published journals he described a moment of mystical awareness that marked a critical turning point in his life as a monk. It occurred during an errand into nearby Louisville, "at the corner of Fourth and Walnut in the center of the shopping district," when he was "suddenly overwhelmed" with the realization that he loved all the people around him. "We could not be alien to one another even though we were total strangers. It was like waking from a dream of separateness, of spurious self-isolation in a special world, the world of renunciation and supposed holiness."

Merton had discovered a sense of solidarity with the human race — not simply in shared sin, but also in grace. "There is no way of telling people that they are all walking around shining like the sun," he wrote. "There are no strangers! . . . The gate of heaven is everywhere."

This experience in Louisville turned out to be a crucial turning point in his life. For years Merton had devoted creative thought to the meaning of monastic and contemplative life. But from this point on he became increasingly concerned with making connections between the monastery and the wider world. Scorn and sarcasm gave way to compassion and

friendship. This was reflected in his writing. Along with the more tradi-
tional spiritual books there appeared articles on war, racism, and other
issues of the day. Long before such positions were commonplace in the
church he was a prophetic voice for peace and nonviolence.

Ironically, this increasing engagement with the world and its prob-
lems was accompanied by an increasing attraction to an even more total
life of contemplation. In 1961 he was given permission to move into
a hermitage on the monastery grounds. There he continued to perfect
the delicate balance between contemplative prayer and openness to the
world that had become the distinctive feature of his spirituality.

In 1968 his abbot allowed him to accept an invitation to address an
international conference of Christian monks in Bangkok. Merton was
particularly excited about the prospect of exploring his deep interest
in Eastern spirituality. On December 10, after delivering his talk, he
retired to his room for a shower and nap. There he was later found
dead, apparently electrocuted by the faulty wiring of a fan.

Thomas Merton is not likely to be canonized. He lived out a model of
holiness that isn't easily pigeonholed in a prefab Catholic mold. And yet
perhaps he represented a type of holiness particularly suited and neces-
sary to our times. Responding to God's call, he let go of his possessions,
his ego, even a spurious kind of "supposed holiness," until he came to
rest in God's emptiness and compassion. It is a story of steadily "putting
off the old person and putting on Christ" — the same process to which all
Christians are called — not for the sake of becoming a different person,
but for the sake of becoming our true selves.

SOLITUDE

There is a silent self within us whose presence is disturbing precisely
because it is so silent: it *can't* be spoken. It has to remain silent. To
articulate it, to verbalize it, is to tamper with it, and in some ways to
destroy it.

Now let us frankly face the fact that our culture is one which is geared
in many ways to help us evade any need to face this inner, silent self. We
live in a state of constant semi-attention to the sound of voices, music,
traffic, or the generalized noise of what goes on around us all the time.
This keeps us immersed in a flood of racket and words, a diffuse medium
in which our consciousness is half diluted: we are not quite "thinking,"
not entirely responding, but we are more or less there. We are not fully

present and not entirely absent; not fully withdrawn, yet not completely available . . . We just float along in the general noise.

All of this can be described as "noise," as commotion and jamming which drown out the deep, secret, and insistent demands of the inner self.

With this inner self we have to come to terms *in silence*. That is the reason for choosing silence. In silence we face and admit the gap between the depths of our being, which we consistently ignore, and the surface which is untrue to our own reality. We recognize the need to be at home with ourselves in order that we may go out to meet others, not just with a mask of affability, but with real commitment and authentic love.

If we are afraid of being alone, afraid of silence, it is perhaps because of our secret despair of inner reconciliation. If we have no hope of being at peace with ourselves in our own personal loneliness and silence, we will never be able to face ourselves at all: we will keep running and never stop. And this flight from the self is . . . a "flight from God." After all, it is in the depths of conscience that God speaks, and if we refuse to open up inside and look into those depths, we also refuse to confront the invisible God who is present within us. This refusal is a partial admission that we do not want God to be God any more than we want ourselves to be our true selves.

Just as we have a superficial, external mask, which we put together with words and actions that do not fully represent all that is in us, so even believers deal with a God who is made up of words, feelings, reassuring slogans, and this is less the God of faith than the product of religious and social routine. Such a "God" can become a substitute for the truth of the invisible God of faith, and though this comforting image may seem real to us, he is really a kind of idol. His chief function is to protect us against a deep encounter with our true inner self and with the true God.

Silence is therefore important even in the life of faith and in our deepest encounter with God. We cannot always be talking, praying words, cajoling, reasoning, or keeping up a kind of devout background music. Much of our well-meant interior religious dialogue is, in fact, a smoke screen and an evasion. Much of it is simply self-reassurance and in the end it is little better than a form of self-justification. Instead of really meeting God in the nakedness of faith in which our inmost being is laid bare before him, we act out an inner ritual that has no function but to allay anxiety.

The purest faith has to be tested by silence in which we listen for the unexpected, in which we are open to what we do not yet know, and in which we slowly and gradually prepare for the day when we will reach out to a new level of being with God. True hope is tested by silence in which we have to wait on the Lord in the obedience of unquestioning faith . . .

Faith demands the integrity of inner trust which produces wholeness, unity, peace, genuine security. Here we see the creative power and fruit- fulness of silence. Not only does silence give us a chance to understand ourselves better, to get a truer and more balanced perspective on our own lives in relation to the lives of others: silence makes us whole if we let it. Silence helps draw together the scattered and dissipated energies of a fragmented existence. It helps us to concentrate on a purpose that really corresponds not only to the deeper needs of our own being but also to God's intentions for us.   — "Creative Silence," *LL,* 40–43

Solitude is not withdrawal from ordinary life. It is not apart from, above, "better than" ordinary life; on the contrary, solitude is the very ground of ordinary life. It is the very ground of that simple, unpretentious, fully human activity by which we quietly earn our daily living and share our experiences with a few intimate friends. But we must learn to know and accept this ground of our being. To most people, though it is always there, it is unthinkable and unknown. Consequently, their life has no center and no foundation. It is dispersed in a pretense of "togetherness" in which there is no real meaning. Only when our activity proceeds out of the ground in which we have consented to be dissolved does it have the divine fruitfulness of love and grace. Only then does it really reach others in true communion. Often our need for others is not love at all but only the need to be sustained in our illusions, even as we sustain others in theirs. But when we have renounced these illusions, then we can certainly go out to others in true compassion. It is in solitude that illusions finally dissolve. But one must work hard to see that they do not reshape themselves in some worse form, peopling our solitude with devils disguised as angels of light. Love, simplicity, and compassion protect us against this. He who is truly alone finds in himself the heart of compas- sion with which to love not only this man or that but all men. He sees them all in the One who is the Word of God, the perfect manifestation of God's Love, Jesus Christ.   — "Love and Solitude," *LL,* 23–24

A man knows when he has found his vocation when he stops thinking about how to live and begins to live. Thus, if one is called to be a solitary, he will stop wondering how he is to live and start living peacefully only when he is in solitude. But if one is not called to a solitary life, the more he is alone the more will he worry about living and forget to live. When we are not living up to our true vocation, thought deadens our life, or substitutes itself for life, or gives in to life so that our life drowns out our thinking and stifles the voice of conscience. When we find our vocation — thought and life are one.

Suppose one has found completeness in his true vocation. Now everything is in unity, in order, at peace. Now work no longer interferes with prayer or prayer with work. Now contemplation no longer needs to be a special "state" that removes one from the ordinary things going on around him for God penetrates all. One does not have to think of giving an account of oneself to anyone but Him.   — TS, 85

CONTEMPLATION

Contemplation is the highest expression of man's intellectual and spiritual life. It is that life itself, fully awake, fully active, fully aware that it is alive. It is spiritual wonder. It is spontaneous awe at the sacredness of life, of being. It is gratitude for life, for awareness and for being. It is a vivid realization of the fact that life and being in us proceed from an invisible, transcendent and infinitely abundant Source. Contemplation is, above all, awareness of the reality of that Source...

Contemplation is also the response to a call: a call from Him Who has no voice, and yet Who speaks in everything that is, and Who, most of all, speaks in the depths of our own being: for we ourselves are words of His. But we are words that are meant to respond to Him, to answer to Him, to echo Him, and even in some way to contain Him and signify Him. Contemplation is this echo...It is as if in creating us God asked a question, and in awakening us to contemplation He answered the question, so that the contemplative is at the same time, question and answer.
                                                                        — NSC, 1, 3

THINGS IN THEIR IDENTITY

A tree gives glory to God by being a tree. For in being what God means it to be it is obeying Him. It "consents," so to speak, to His creative love. It is expressing an idea which is in God and which is not distinct from the essence of God, and therefore a tree imitates God by being a tree.

The more a tree is like itself, the more it is like Him. If it tried to be like something else which it was never intended to be, it would be less like God and therefore it would give Him less glory.

No two created beings are exactly alike. And their individuality is no imperfection. On the contrary, the perfection of each created thing is not merely in its conformity to an abstract type but in its own individual identity with itself...

Therefore each particular being, in its individuality, its concrete nature and entity, with all its own characteristics and its private qualities and its own inviolable identity, gives glory to God by being precisely what He wants it to be here and now, in the circumstances ordained for it by His Love and His infinite Art.

The forms and individual characters of living and growing things, of inanimate beings, of animals and flowers and all nature, constitute their holiness in the sight of God...

The pale flowers of the dogwood outside this window are saints. The little yellow flowers that nobody notices on the edge of that road are saints looking up into the face of God...

The lakes hidden among the hills are saints, and the sea too is a saint who praises God without interruption in her majestic dance.

But what about you? What about me?...

For me to be a saint means to be myself. Therefore the problem of sanctity and salvation is in fact the problem of finding out who I am and of discovering my true self.

Trees and animals have no problem. God makes them what they are without consulting them, and they are perfectly satisfied.

With us it is different. God leaves us free to be whatever we like. We can be ourselves or not, as we please. We are at liberty to be real, or to be unreal. We may be true or false, the choice is ours. We may wear now one mask and now another, and never, if we so desire, appear with our own true face. But we cannot make these choices with impunity. Causes have effects, and if we lie to ourselves and to others, then we cannot expect to find truth and reality whenever we happen to want them. If we have chosen the way of falsity we must not be surprised that truth eludes us when we finally come to need it!

The seeds that are planted in my liberty at every moment, by God's will, are the seeds of my own identity, my reality, my own happiness, my own sanctity.

To refuse them is to refuse everything; it is the refusal of my own existence and being: of my identity, my very self.

Not to accept and love and do God's will is to refuse the fullness of my existence...

All sin starts from the assumption that my false sense, the self that exists only in my own egocentric desires, is the fundamental reality of life to which everything else in the universe is ordered...

The secret of my identity is hidden in the love and mercy of God.

But whatever is in God is really identical with Him, for His infinite simplicity admits no division and no distinction. Therefore I cannot hope to find myself anywhere except in Him.

Ultimately the only way that I can be myself is to become identified with Him in Whom is hidden the reason and fulfillment of my existence.

Therefore there is only one problem on which all my existence, my peace and my happiness depend: to discover myself in discovering God. If I find Him I will find myself and if I find my true self I will find Him.

—*NSC, 29–36*

THE PLASTER SAINT

A very wise piece of advice, which St. Benedict gives to monks in his Rule, is that they should not desire to be called saints before they are holy, but that they should first become saints in order that their reputation for holiness may be based on reality. This brings out the great difference between real spiritual perfection and man's idea of perfection. Or perhaps one might say, more accurately, the difference between sanctity and narcissism...

The stereotyped image [of the saint] is easy to sketch out here: it is essentially an image without the slightest moral flaw. The saint, if he ever sinned at all, eventually became impeccable after a perfect conversion. Impeccability not being quite enough, he is raised beyond the faintest possibility of feeling temptation...His words are always the most edifying clichés...They are without humor as they are without wonder, without feeling, and without interest in the common affairs of mankind...

Until we realize that before a man can become a saint he must first of all be a *man* in all the humanity and fragility of man's actual condition, we will never be able to understand the meaning of the word "saint." Not only were all the saints perfectly human, not only did their sanctity enrich and deepen their humanity, but the Holiest of all the Saints, the Incarnate Word, Jesus Christ, was himself the most deeply and perfectly human being who ever lived on the face of the earth...

Hence sanctity is not a matter of being *less* human, but *more* human than other men. This implies a greater capacity for concern, for suffering, for understanding, for sympathy, and also for humor, for joy, for appreciation of the good and beautiful things of life...

The true saint is not one who has become convinced that he himself is holy, but one who is overwhelmed by the realization that God, and God alone, is holy. He is so awestruck with the reality of the divine holiness that he begins to see it everywhere.   —*LH,* 22–26

CHRIST AND THE WORLD

Whether or not a major war...should finally break, we have to live in a way that daily takes this possibility seriously into account.

This implies certain important choices, certain preferences.

Even though one may not be able to halt the race toward death, one must nevertheless *choose life,* and the things that favor life. This means respect for every living thing, but especially for every man, made in the image of God. Respect for man even in his blindness and in his confusion, even when he may do evil. For we must see that the meaning of man has been totally changed by the Crucifixion. Every man is Christ on the Cross, whether he realizes it or not. But we, if we are Christians, must learn to realize it. That is what it means to be a Christian: not simply one who believes certain reports about Christ, but one who lives in a *conscious confrontation with Christ* in himself and in other men.

—*CGB,* 219

As usual, one comes back to the old question: what do you mean by "the world" anyway? In this, I don't think an abstract answer makes too much sense. My concrete answer is: what did I leave when I entered the monastery? As far as I can see, what I abandoned when I "left the world" and came to the monastery was the *understanding of myself* that I had developed in the context of civil society — my identification with what appeared to me to be its aims...Many of these were trivial, some of them were onerous, all are closely related. The image of a society that is happy because it drinks Coca-Cola or Seagrams or both and is protected by the bomb. The society that is imaged in the mass media and in advertising, in the movies, in TV, in best-sellers, in current fads, in all the pompous and trifling masks, with which it hides callousness, sensuality, hypocrisy, cruelty, and fear. Is this "the world" Yes. It is the same wherever you have mass man...

For my own part, I am by my whole life committed to a certain protest and nonacquiescence, and that is why I am a monk. Yet I know that protest is not enough — is perhaps meaningless. Yet that is also why protest and nonacquiescence must extend to certain conceptions of monasticism which seem to me to be simply a fancy-dress adaptation of what we are claiming we have renounced.

As if, for instance, "leaving the world" were adequately summed up by those pictures of "the Trappist" with his cowl over his head and his back to the camera, looking at a lake.   — CGB, 47–48

There is only one true flight from the world; it is not an escape from conflict, anguish and suffering, but the flight from disunity and separation, to unity and peace in the love of other men.

What is the "world" that Christ would not pray for, and of which He said that His disciples were in it but not of it? The world is the unquiet city of those who live for themselves and are therefore divided against one another in a struggle that cannot end, for it will go on eternally in hell. It is the city of those who are fighting for possession of limited things and for the monopoly of goods and pleasures that cannot be shared by all.

But if you try to escape from this world merely by leaving the city and hiding yourself in solitude, you will only take the city with you into solitude; and yet you can be entirely out of the world while remaining in the midst of it, if you let God set you free from your own selfishness and if you live for love alone.

For the flight from the world is nothing else but the flight from self-concern. And the man who locks himself up in private with his own selfishness has put himself into a position where the evil within him will either possess him like a devil or drive him out of his head.

That is why it is dangerous to go into solitude merely because you like to be alone.   — NSC, 78–79

LETTER TO A PEACEMAKER

Do not depend on the hope of results. When you are doing the sort of work you have taken on, essentially an apostolic work, you may have to face the fact that your work will be apparently worthless and even achieve no results at all, if not perhaps results opposite to what you expect. As you get used to this idea you start more and more to concentrate not on the results but on the value, the rightness, the truth of the work itself. And there too a great deal has to be gone through, as gradually you struggle less and less for an idea and more and more for specific people. The range tends to narrow down, but it gets much more real. In the end, it is the reality of personal relationships that saves everything.

You are fed up with words, and I don't blame you. I am nauseated by them sometimes. I am also, to tell the truth, nauseated with ideals and with causes. This sounds like heresy, but I think you will understand what I mean. It is so easy to get engrossed with ideas and slogans and myths that in the end one is left holding the bag, empty, with no trace of meaning left in it. And then the temptation is to yell louder than ever in order to make the meaning be there again by magic . . .

As for the big results, these are not in your hands or mine, but they can suddenly happen, and we can share in them: but there is no point in building our lives on this personal satisfaction, which may be denied us and which after all is not that important.

The next step in the process is for you to see that your own thinking about what you are doing is crucially important. You are probably striving to build yourself an identity in your work and your witness. You are using it, so to speak, to protect yourself against nothingness, annihilation. That is not the right use of your work. All the good that you will do will come not from you but from the fact that you have allowed yourself, in the obedience of faith, to be used by God's love. Think of this more and gradually you will be free from the need to prove yourself, and you can be more open to the power that will work through you without your knowing it.

The great thing after all is to live, not to pour out your life in the service of a myth: and we turn the best things into myths. If you can get free from the domination of causes and just serve Christ's truth, you will be able to do more and will be less crushed by the inevitable disappointments . . .

The real hope, then, is not in something we think we can do, but in God who is making something good out of it in some way we cannot see. If we can do His will, we will be helping in this process. But we will not necessarily know all about it beforehand.

—Letter to Jim Forest, February 21, 1965, *HGL*, 294–97

SHINING LIKE THE SUN

In Louisville, at the corner of Fourth and Walnut, in the center of the shopping district, I was suddenly overwhelmed with the realization that I loved all those people, that they were mine and I theirs, that we could not be alien to one another even though we were total strangers. It was like waking from a dream of separateness, of spurious self-isolation in a special world, the world of renunciation and supposed holiness. The whole illusion of a separate holy existence is a dream. Not that I question the reality of my vocation, or of my monastic life: but the conception of "separation from the world" that we have in the monastery too easily presents itself as a complete illusion: the illusion that by making vows we have become a different species of being, pseudo-angels, "spiritual men," men of interior life, what have you...

This sense of liberation from an illusory difference was such a relief and such a joy to me that I almost laughed out loud. And I suppose my happiness could have taken form in the words: "Thank God, thank God that I *am* like other men, that I am only a man among others."...

It is a glorious destiny to be a member of the human race, though it is a race dedicated to many absurdities and one which makes many terrible mistakes: yet, with all that, God Himself gloried in becoming a member of the human race. A member of the human race! To think that such a commonplace realization should suddenly seem like news that one holds the winning ticket in a cosmic sweepstake.

I have the immense joy of being *man*, a member of a race in which God Himself became incarnate. As if the sorrows and stupidities of the human condition could overwhelm me, now I realize what we all are. And if only everybody could realize this! But it cannot be explained. There is no way of telling people that they are all walking around shining like the sun.

This changes nothing in the sense and value of my solitude, for it is in fact the function of solitude to make one realize such things with a clarity that would be impossible to anyone completely immersed in the other cares, the other illusions, and all the automatisms of a tightly collective existence. My solitude, however, is not my own, for I see now how much it belongs to them — and that I have a responsibility for it in their regard, not just in my own. It is because I am one with them that I owe it to them to be alone, and when I am alone they are not "they" but my own self. There are no strangers!

Then it was as if I suddenly saw the secret beauty of their hearts, the depths of their hearts where neither sin nor desire nor self-knowledge can reach, the core of their reality, the person that each one is in God's eyes. If only they could all see themselves as they really *are*. If only we could see each other that way all the time. There would be no more war, no more hatred, no more cruelty, no more greed...I suppose the big problem would be that we would fall down and worship each other. But this cannot be *seen*, only believed and "understood" by a peculiar gift.

Again, that expression, *le point vierge* (I cannot translate it) comes in here. At the center of our being is a point of nothingness which is untouched by sin and by illusion, a point of pure truth, a point or spark which belongs entirely to God, which is never at our disposal, from which God disposes of our minds, which is inaccessible to the fantasies of our own mind or the brutalities of our own will. This little point of nothingness and of *absolute poverty* is the pure glory of God in us. It is so to speak His name written in us, as our poverty, as our indigence, as our dependence, as our sonship. It is like a pure diamond, blazing with the invisible light of heaven. It is in everybody, and if we could see it we would see these billions of points of light coming together in the face and blaze of a sun that would make all the darkness and cruelty of life vanish completely...I have no program for this seeing. It is only given. But the gate of heaven is everywhere.   —*CGB*, 156–58

When I wrote [*The Seven Storey Mountain*] the fact uppermost in my mind was that I had seceded from the world of my time in all clarity and with total freedom. The break and the secession were, to me, matters of the greatest importance. Hence the somewhat negative tone of so many parts of this book.

Since that time, I have learned, I believe, to look back into that world with greater compassion, seeing those in it not as alien to myself, not as peculiar and deluded strangers, but as identified with myself. In breaking from "their world" I have strangely broken from them. In freeing myself from their delusions and preoccupations I have identified myself, none the less, with their struggles and their blind, desperate hope of happiness.

But precisely because I am identified with them, I must refuse all the more definitively to make their delusions my own. I must refuse their ideology of matter, power, quantity, movement, activism, and force. I reject this because I see it to be the source and the expression of the spiritual hell which man has made of his world: the hell which has burst into flame in two total wars of incredible horror, the hell of spiritual emptiness and sub-human fury which has resulted in crimes like Auschwitz and Hiroshima. This I can and must reject with all the power of my being. This all sane men seek to reject. But the question is: how can one sincerely reject the effect if he continues to embrace the cause?

My conversion to the Christian faith, or to be precise, my conversion to Christ, is something I have always regarded as a radical liberation from the delusions and obsessions of modern man and his society. I have always believed and continue to believe that faith is the only real protection against the absorption of freedom and intelligence in the crass and thoughtless servitude of mass society. Religious faith, and faith alone, can open the inner ground of man's being to the liberty of the sons of God, and preserve him from the surrender of his integrity to the seduction of a totalitarian life...Man must believe in something and that in which he believes becomes his god. To serve some material or human entity as one's god is to be a slave of that which perishes, and thus to be a slave of death, sorrow, falsehood, misery. The only true liberty is in the service of that which is beyond all limits, beyond all definitions, beyond all human appreciation: that which is All...

The monastery is not an "escape" from the world. On the contrary, by being in the monastery I take my true part in all the struggles and sufferings of the world. To adopt a life that is essentially non-assertive, non-violent, a life of humility and peace is in itself a statement of one's position. But each one in such a life can, by the personal modality of his decision, give his whole life a special orientation. It is my intention to make my entire life a rejection of, a protest against the crimes and injustices of war and political tyranny which threaten to destroy the whole race of man and the world with him. By my monastic life and vows I am saying NO to all the concentration camps, the aerial bombardments, the staged political trials, the judicial murders, the radical injustices, the economic tyrannies, and the whole socio-economic apparatus which seems geared for nothing but global destruction in spite of all its fair words in favor of peace. I make monastic silence a protest against the lies of politicians, propagandists and agitators, and when I speak it is to deny that my faith and my Church can ever seriously be aligned with these forces of injustice and destruction...

If I say NO to all these secular forces, I also say YES to all that is good in the world and in man. I say YES to all that is beautiful in nature, and in order that this may be the yes of freedom and not of subjection, I must refuse to possess anything in the world purely as my own. I say YES to all the men and women who are my brothers and sisters in the world, but for this yes to be an assent of freedom and not of subjection, I must live so that no one of them may seem to belong to me, and that I may not belong to any of them. It is because I want to be more to them than a friend that I become, to all of them, a stranger.

—Preface to the Japanese edition of
The Seven Storey Mountain (1963), HR, 43–46

A LETTER ON THE CONTEMPLATIVE LIFE

Let us suppose the message of a so-called contemplative to a so-called man of the world to be something like this:

My dear Brother, first of all, I apologize for addressing you when you have not addressed me and have not really asked me anything. And I apologize for being behind a high wall which you do not understand. This high wall is to you a problem, and perhaps it is also a problem to me, O my brother. Perhaps you ask me why I stay behind it out of obedience? Perhaps you are no longer satisfied with the reply that if I stay behind this wall I have quiet, recollection, tranquility of heart. Perhaps you ask me what right I have to all this peace and tranquility when some sociologists have estimated that within the lifetime of our younger generations a private room will become an unheard-of luxury. I do not have a satisfactory answer... It is true that when I came to this monastery where I am, I came in revolt against the meaningless confusion of a life in which there was so much activity, so much movement, so much useless talk, so much superficial and needless stimulation, that I could not remember who I was.

But the fact remains that my flight from the world is not a reproach to you who remain in the world, and I have no right to repudiate the world in a purely negative fashion, because if I do that my flight will have taken me not to truth and to God but to a private, though doubtless pious illusion.

Can I tell you that I have found answers to the questions that torment the man of our time? I do not know if I have found answers. When I first became a monk, yes, I was more sure of "answers." But as I grow old in the monastic life and advance further into solitude, I become aware that I have only begun to seek the questions, And what are the questions? Can man make sense out of existence? Can man honestly give his life meaning merely by adopting a certain set of explanations which pretend to tell him why the world began and where it will end, why there is evil and what is necessary for a good life? My brother, perhaps in my solitude I have become as it were an explorer for you, a searcher in realms which you are not able to visit — except perhaps in the company of your psychiatrist. I have been summoned to explore a desert area of man's heart in which the explanations no longer suffice, and in which one learns that only experience counts. An arid, rocky, dark land of the soul, sometimes illuminated by strange fires which men fear and peopled by specters which men studiously avoid except in their nightmares. And in this area I have learned that one cannot truly know hope unless he has found out how like despair hope is. The language of Christianity has said this for centuries in other less naked terms. But the language of Christianity has been so used and so misused that sometimes you distrust it: you do not know whether or not behind the word "cross" there stands the experience of mercy and salvation, or only the threat of punishment. If my word means anything to you, I can say to you that I have experienced the cross to mean mercy and not cruelty, truth and not deception; that the news of the truth and love of Jesus is indeed the true good news, but in our time it speaks out in strange places. And perhaps it speaks out in you more than it does in me; perhaps Christ is nearer to you than he is to me. This I say without shame or guilt because I have learned to rejoice that Jesus is in the world in people who know Him not, that He is at work in them when they think themselves far from Him, and it is my joy to tell you to hope though you think that for you of all men hope is impossible. Hope not because you think you can be good, but because God loves us irrespective of our merits and whatever is good in us comes from His love, not from our own doing. Hope because Jesus is with those who are poor and outcast and perhaps despised even by those who should seek them and care for them more lovingly because they act in God's name ... No one on earth has reason to despair of Jesus, because Jesus loves man, loves him in his sin, and we too must love man in his sin ...

O my brother, the contemplative is not the man who has fiery visions of the cherubim carrying God on their imagined chariot, but simply he who has risked his mind in the desert beyond language and beyond ideas where God is encountered in the nakedness of pure trust, that is to say in the surrender of our own poverty and incompleteness in order no longer to clench our minds in a cramp upon themselves, as if thinking made us exist. The message of hope the contemplative offers you, then, Brother, is not that you need to find your way through the jungle of language and problems that today surround God; but that whether you understand or not, God loves you, is present to you, lives in you, dwells in you, calls you, saves you, and offers you an understanding and light which are like nothing you ever found in books or heard in sermons. The contemplative has nothing to tell you except to reassure you and say that if you dare to penetrate your own silence and dare to advance without fear into the solitude of your own heart, and risk the sharing of that solitude with the lonely other who seeks God through you and with you, then you will truly recover the light and the capacity to understand what is beyond words and beyond explanations because it is too close to be explained: it is the intimate union in the depths of your own heart, of God's spirit and your own secret inmost self, so that you and He are in all truth One Spirit. I love you, in Christ . . .

Yours in Christ Jesus,
Br. M. Louis
(Thomas Merton)
— *MJ*, 170–73

PRAYER

My Lord God, I have no idea where I am going. I do not see the road ahead of me. I cannot know for certain where it will end. Nor do I really know myself, and the fact that I think I am following your will does not mean that I am actually doing so. But I believe that the desire to please you does in fact please you. And I hope I have that desire in all that I am doing. I hope that I will never do anything apart from that desire. And I know that if I do this you will lead me by the right road, though I may know nothing about it. Therefore I will trust you always though I may seem to be lost and in the shadow of death. I will not fear, for you are ever with me, and you will never leave me to face my perils alone.   — *TS*, 81

SOURCES

CGB   *Conjectures of a Guilty Bystander* (Garden City, NY: Doubleday, 1966).

HGL   *The Hidden Ground of Love: The Letters of Thomas Merton on Religious Experience and Social Concerns,* ed. William H. Shannon (New York: Farrar, Strasus & Giroux, 1985).

HR   *Honorable Reader: Reflections on My Work,* ed. Robert
          Daggy (New York: Crossroad, 1991).

LH   *Life and Holiness* (New York: Herder, 1963).

LL   *Love and Living,* ed. Naomi Burton Stone and Brother
          Patrick Hart (New York: Farrar Straus Giroux, 1979).

MJ   *The Monastic Journey,* ed. Brother Patrick Hart (Kansas City:
          Sheed Andrews and McMeel, Inc., 1977).

NSC   *New Seeds of Contemplation* (New York: New Directions,
          1961).

TS   *Thoughts in Solitude* (New York: Farrar Straus, 1958).

See also: *Thomas Merton: Essential Writings,* ed. Christine Bochen
(Maryknoll, NY: Orbis Books, 2000).

TWO

MOTHER TERESA
OF CALCUTTA

Serving Jesus in His Distressing Disguise

⊡⊡⊡⊡⊡⊡⊡⊡

On September 10, 1945, the woman who would become Mother Teresa was traveling on a train to Darjeeling, a hill station in the Himalayas. At the time she was simply Sister Agnes, a thirty-six-year-old Loreto Sister of Albanian extraction, who had spent the past twenty years teaching in her order's schools in India. Though she was a devoted nun, beloved by her mostly middle-class students, there was nothing to suggest that she would one day be regarded as one of the most compelling Christian witnesses of the twentieth century. But on this day she received "a call within a call." God, she suddenly felt, wanted something more from her: "He wanted me to be poor with the poor and to love him in the distressing disguise of the poorest of the poor."

So, with the permission of her congregation, she left her convent. In place of her traditional religious habit she donned a simple white sari with blue border and went out to seek Jesus in the desperate byways of Calcutta. Eventually she was joined by others — including many of her former students. They became the Missionaries of Charity. And she became Mother Teresa.

With time Mother Teresa would establish centers of service around the globe for the sick, the homeless, the unwanted. But she was particularly identified with her home for the dying in Calcutta. There, destitute and dying men and women, gathered off the streets of the city, were welcomed to receive loving care and respect until they died. Those who had lived like "animals in the gutter" were enabled, in Mother Teresa's home, to "die like angels" — knowing that they were truly valued and loved as precious children of God.

23

It was not Mother Teresa's way to change social structures. "We are not social workers," she said, but "contemplatives in the heart of the world. For we are touching the body of Christ twenty-four hours a day." It was this mystical insight, which she obviously lived, that made Mother Teresa such a widely inspiring figure. She did not simply practice charity; she embodied it.

For many years Mother Teresa toiled in obscurity. But eventually she was "discovered" by the world. She became the subject of documentary films and biographies; she received honorary degrees from prestigious universities and countless honors, including the Nobel Peace Prize for 1979. Widely regarded as a "living saint," she nevertheless remained remarkably unburdened by such adulation. Nor did she have any exalted sense of her own vocation. "We can do no great things," she said, "only small things with great love." Often when people begged to join her in her "wonderful work" in Calcutta she would respond gently but firmly, "Find your own Calcutta!"

In later life Mother Teresa traveled widely around the world. In the affluent West she had no trouble finding poverty — both the material kind and a no less destructive impoverishment of the spirit. The answer in both cases was love, a love that would begin with persons and ultimately transform the world. But before we tried to love the entire world, we should start by trying to love one other person — someone apparently unlovable, unwanted, or rejected. "You can save only one at a time. We can love one at a time." That, she believed, is what we were put on earth to do: "Something beautiful for God."

Mother Teresa's life ended on September 5, 1997. But that was not the end of her witness. She was beatified with unusual speed in 2003. Four years later her personal diaries were published, revealing the spiritual desolation she had suffered over a period of fifty years. "In my own soul, I feel the terrible pain of [the loss of God]. I feel that God does not want me, that God is not God and that he does not really exist." Apparently, after the experience of her intimate "call" from God on the train to Darjeeling — a call so powerful that it sustained her for the rest of her life — she went on to suffer excruciatingly from a sense of God's absence and silence. And yet she continued to live out her faith with extraordinary dedication.

It seems she had prayed at one point to experience the depth of Jesus' own suffering — especially the desolation of his abandonment in the Garden of Gethsemane and on the Cross. With the help of her spiritual *advisor, she came to see that her own sufferings were an answer to that prayer — a form of intimacy with Jesus, and a distinctive dimension of her vocation. Did this experience help to insulate her from the adulation of the world? Did it intensify her identification with those who were otherwise dejected and abandoned?*

As her spiritual advisor counseled, she should see her craving for God as a sign that she was not truly abandoned. This "absence" was a paradoxical sign of God's presence in her life. In response to this counsel, she wrote, "I can't express in words — the gratitude I owe you for your kindness to me — for the first time in...years — I have come to love the darkness." And she considered that this might be part of her lasting witness to the world — to strengthen the faith and hope of others who felt similarly lost and abandoned. "If I ever become a Saint," she wrote, "I will surely be one of 'darkness.' I will continually be absent from Heaven — to [light] the light of those in darkness on earth."

HOW TO PRAY

It was the apostles who asked Jesus: "Jesus, teach us how to pray" — because they saw him so often pray and they knew that he was talking to his Father. What those hours of prayer must have been — we know only from that continual love of Jesus for his Father. "My Father!" And he taught his disciples a very simple way of talking to God himself.

Before Jesus came God was great in his majesty, great in his creation. And then when Jesus came he become one of us, because his Father loved the world so much that he gave his Son. And Jesus loved his Father and he wanted us to learn to pray by loving one another as the Father has loved him.

"I love you," he kept on saying, "as the Father loved you, love him." And his love was the cross, his love was the bread of life. And he wants us to pray with a clean heart, with a simple heart, with a humble heart. "Unless you become little children, you cannot learn to pray, you cannot enter heaven, you cannot see God." To become a little child means to be one with the Father, to love the Father, to be at peace with the Father, our Father.

Prayer is nothing but that being in the family, being one with the Father in the Son to the Holy Spirit. The love of the Father for his Son — the Holy Spirit. And the love, our love for the Father, through Jesus, his Son, filled with the Holy Spirit, is our union with God and the fruit of that union with God, the fruit of that prayer — what we call prayer. We have given that name but actually prayer is nothing but that oneness with Christ.

As St. Paul has said, "I live no longer I, but Christ lives in me." Christ prays in me, Christ works in me, Christ thinks of me, Christ looks through my eyes, Christ speaks through my words, Christ works with my hands, Christ walks with my feet, Christ loves with my heart. As St. Paul's prayer was, "I belong to Christ and nothing will separate me from the love of Christ." It was that oneness: oneness with God, oneness with the Master in the Holy Spirit.

And if we really want to pray we must first learn to listen, for in the silence of the heart God speaks. And to be able to hear that silence, to be able to hear God we need a clean heart, for a clean heart can see God, can hear God, can listen to God, and then only from the fullness of our heart can we speak to God. But we cannot speak unless we have listened, unless we have made that connection with God in the silence of our heart.

And so prayer is not meant to be a torture, not meant to make us feel uneasy, is not meant to trouble us. It is something to look forward to, to talk to my Father, to talk to Jesus, the one to whom I belong: body, soul, mind, heart.

And when times come when we can't pray, it is very simple: if Jesus is in my heart let him pray, let me allow him to pray in me, to talk to his Father in the silence of my heart. Since I cannot speak — he will speak; since I cannot pray — he will pray. That's why often we should say: "Jesus in my heart, I believe in your faithful love for me, I love you." And often we should be in that unity with him and allow him, and when we have nothing to give — let us give him that nothingness. When we cannot pray — let us give that inability to him. There is one more reason to let him pray in us to the Father. Let us ask him to pray in us, for no one knows the Father better than he. No one can pray better than Jesus. And if my heart is pure, if in my heart Jesus is alive, if my heart is a tabernacle of the living God to sanctify in grace: Jesus and I are one. He prays in me, he thinks in me, he works with me and through me, he uses my tongue to speak, he uses my brain to think, he uses my hands to touch him in the broken body.

And for us who have the precious gift of Holy Communion every day, that contact with Christ is our prayer; that love for Christ, that joy in his presence, that surrender to his love for Christ, that joy in his presence, that surrender to his love is our prayer. For prayer is nothing but that complete surrender, complete oneness with Christ.

And this is what makes us contemplatives in the heart of the world; for we are twenty-four hours then in his presence: in the hungry, in the naked, in the homeless, in the unwanted, unloved, uncared for; for Jesus said: Whatever you do to the least of my brethren, you do it to me."

Therefore doing it to him, we are praying the work; for in doing it with him, doing it for him, doing it to him we are loving him; and in loving him we come more and more into that oneness with him and we allow him to live his life in us. And this living of Christ in us is holiness.

— Excerpted from talk of June 8, 1980, Berlin, *SV*, 495–97

Spend your time in prayer. If you pray you will have faith, and if you have faith you will naturally want to serve. The one who prays cannot but have faith, and when you have faith you want to put it into action. Faith in action is service. Faith in action becomes a delight because it gives you the opportunity of putting your love for Christ into action — it is meeting Christ, serving Christ. — *TS*, 112

Prayer, to be fruitful, must come from the heart and must be able to touch the heart of God. See how Jesus taught his disciples to pray. Call God your Father; praise and glorify his name. Do his will as the saints do it in heaven; ask for daily bread; spiritual and temporal; ask for forgiveness of your own sins and that you may forgive others, and also for the grace not to give in to temptations and for the final grace to be delivered from the evil that is in us and around us. — *JWS*, 3

CONTEMPLATION

We must join our prayer with work. We try to bring this across to our sisters by inviting them to make their work a prayer. How is it possible to change one's work into a prayer? Work cannot substitute for prayer. Nevertheless, we can learn to make work a prayer. How can we do this? By doing our work with Jesus and for Jesus. That is the way to make our work a prayer. It is possible that I may not be able to keep my attention fully on God while I work, but God doesn't demand that I do so. Yet I can fully desire and intend that my work be done with Jesus and for

Jesus. This is beautiful and that is what God wants. He wants our will
and our desire to be for him, for our family, for our children, for our
brethren, and for the poor.   —OHFL, 58

By contemplation the soul draws directly from the heart of God the
graces that the active life must distribute.

We [the Missionaries of Charity] are called to be contemplatives in
the heart of the world by:

Seeking the face of God in everything, everyone, everywhere, all the
time, and his hand in every happening;

Seeing and adoring the presence of Jesus, especially in the lowly
appearance of bread, and in the distressing disguise of the poor.

Our life of contemplation must retain the following characteristics:

Being missionaries: by going out physically or in spirit in search of
souls all over the world.

Being contemplatives: by gathering the whole world at the very center
of our hearts where the Lord abides, and allowing the pure water of
divine grace to flow plentifully and unceasingly from the source itself,
on the whole of his creation.

Being universal: by praying and contemplating with all and for all,
especially with and for the spiritually poorest of the poor.

Another aspect of our life of contemplation is simplicity, which makes
us see the face of God in everything, everyone, everywhere, all the time,
and his hand in all the happenings; and makes us do all that we do —
whether we think, study, work, speak, eat, or take our rest — under the
loving gaze of the Father, being totally available to him in any form he
may come to us.

What is contemplation? To live the life of Jesus. This is what I understand — to love Jesus, to live his life in us, to live our life in his life.
That's contemplation. We must have a clean heart to be able to see: no
jealousy, anger, contention, and especially no uncharitableness...

To me, contemplation is not to be shut up in a dark place but to allow
Jesus to live his passion, love and humility in us, praying with us, being
with us, sanctifying through us.   —HW, 333–35

These two lives, action and contemplation, instead of excluding each
other, call for each other's help, implement and complete each other.
Action, to be productive, has need of contemplation. The latter, when

it gets to a certain degree of intensity, diffuses some of its excess on the first. By contemplation the soul draws directly from the heart of God the graces which the active life must distribute.   —*JWS*, 8

The true interior life makes the active life burn forth and consume everything. It makes us find Jesus in the dark holes of the slums, in the most pitiful miseries of the poor — the God-Man naked on the cross, mournful, despised by all, the man of suffering crushed like a worm by the scourging and the crucifixion. This interior life motivates the Missionary of Charity to serve Jesus in the poor.   —*TS*, 117

VOCATION

At Loreto I was the happiest nun in the world. Leaving the work I did there was a great sacrifice. What I did not have to leave was being a religious sister.

The Sisters of Loreto were devoted to teaching, which is a genuine apostolate for Christ. But my specific vocation, within the religious vocation, was for the poorest poor. It was a call from inside my vocation — like a second vocation. It was a command to resign Loreto, where I was happy, in order to serve the poor in the streets.

In 1946, when I was going by train to Darjeeling for some spiritual exercises, I sensed a call to renounce everything in order to follow Christ in the poor suburbs to serve among the poorest poor. I knew that God wanted something from me.   —*HJ*, 39–40

In the world there are some who struggle for justice and human rights. We have no time for this because we are in daily and continuous contact with men who are starving for a piece of bread to put in their mouth and for some affection. Should I devote myself to struggle for the justice of tomorrow or even for the justice of today, the most needy people would die right in front of me because they lack a glass of milk.

Nevertheless, I want to state clearly that I do not condemn those who struggle for justice. I believe there are different options for the people of God. To me the most important is to serve the neediest people.

Within the church some do one thing, others do a different thing. What is important is that all of us remain united, each one of us developing his own specific task.   —*HJ*, 113–14

We all have the duty to serve God where we are called to do so. I feel
called to serve individuals, to love each human being. My calling is not
to judge the institutions. I am not qualified to condemn anyone. I never
think in terms of a crowd, but of individual persons.

If I thought in terms of crowds, I would never begin my work.

I believe in the personal touch of one to one.

If others are convinced that God wants them to change social
structures, that is a matter for them to take up with God.   — OW, 99

GOD'S DISGUISE

We have the specific task of giving material and spiritual help to the
poorest of the poor, not only the ones in the slums but those who live in
any corner of the world as well.

To do this, we make ourselves live the love of God in prayer and in
our work, through a life characterized by the simplicity and humility of
the Gospel. We do this by loving Jesus in the bread of the Eucharist, and
loving and serving him hidden under the painful guise of the poorest of
the poor, whether their poverty is a material poverty or a spiritual one.
We do this by recognizing in them (and giving back to them) the image
and likeness of God.   — OW, 108

If sometimes our poor people have had to die of starvation it is not
because God didn't care for them, but because you and I didn't give,
were not instruments of love in the hands of God, to give them that
bread, to give them that clothing; because we did not recognize him,
when once more Christ came in distressing disguise — in the hungry
man, in the lonely man, in the homeless child, and seeking for shelter.

God has identified himself with the hungry, the sick, the naked, the
homeless; hunger, not only for bread, but for love, for care, to be somebody to someone; nakedness, not of clothing only, but nakedness of that
compassion that very few people give to the unknown; homelessness, not
only just for a shelter made of stone, but that homelessness that comes
from having no one to call your own.   — GG, 24–25

Hungry for love, He looks at you. Thirsty for kindness, He begs of you.
Naked for loyalty, He hopes in you. Homeless for shelter in your heart,
He asks of you. Will you be that one to Him?   — HW, 56

The important thing is not to do a lot or to do everything. The important thing is to be ready for anything, at all times; to be convinced that when serving the poor, we really serve God. — *OW*, 29

LOVE

Love — really be a contemplative in the heart of the world. Whatever you do, even if you help somebody cross the road, you do it to Jesus. Even giving somebody a glass of water, you do it to Jesus. Such simple little teaching, but it is more and more important. — *JWS*, 73

"Thou shalt love the Lord thy God with thy whole heart, with thy whole soul, and with thy whole mind." This is the commandment of the great God, and he cannot command the impossible. Love is a fruit in season at all times, and within reach of every hand. Anyone may gather it and no limit is set. Everyone can reach this love through meditation, the spirit of prayer, and sacrifice, by an intense inner life...

There is no limit, because God is love and love is God, and so you are really in love with God. And then, God's love is infinite. But part is to love and to give until it hurts. And that's why it's not how much you do, but how much love you put into the action. How much love we put in our presents. That's why people — maybe they are very rich people — who have not got a capacity to give and to receive love are the poorest of the poor. And I think this is what our sisters have got — the spreading of joy that you see in many religious people who have given themselves without reserve to God...

Our work is only the expression of the love we have for God. We have to pour our love on someone, and the people are the means of expressing our love for God. — *GG*, 67–68

To show great love for God and our neighbor we need not do great things. It is how much love we put in the doing that makes our offering something beautiful for God. — *GG*, 69

The words of Jesus, "Love one another as I have loved you," must be not only a light for us but a flame that consumes the self in us. Love, in order to survive, must be nourished by sacrifices, especially the sacrifice of self.

Suffering is nothing by itself. But suffering shared with the passion of Christ is a wonderful gift, the most beautiful gift, a token of love...

I must be willing to give whatever it takes to do good to others. This requires that I be willing to give until it hurts. Otherwise, there is no true love in me and I bring injustice, not peace, to those around me.

—*HW*, 48–49

At the time of death, when we meet God face-to-face, we will be judged concerning love, concerning how much we have loved. Not concerning how much we have accomplished, but rather how much love we have put into what we have done.

In order for love to be genuine, it has to be above all a love for my neighbor. Love for my neighbor will lead me to true love for God. What the sisters, the brothers, and the co-workers try to do all over the world is to put into loving action their love for God.   —*HJ*, 114–15

POVERTY

Christ being rich emptied himself. This is where contradiction lies. If I want to be poor like Christ — who became poor even though he was rich — I must do the same. Nowadays people want to be poor and live with the poor, but they want to be free to dispose of things as they wish. To have this freedom is to be rich. They want both and they cannot have both. This is another kind of contradiction.

Our poverty is our freedom. This is our poverty — the giving up of our freedom to dispose of things, to choose, to possess. The moment I use and dispose of things as mine, that moment I cease to be poor.

We must strive to acquire the true spirit of poverty which manifests itself in a love for the practice of the virtue of poverty in imitation of Christ — in imitation of him who chose it as the compassion of his life on earth when he came to live among us. Christ did not have to lead a life of poverty. Thus he taught us how important it is for our sanctification.

—*TS*, 56–57

There are many kinds of poverty. Even in countries where the economic situation seems to be a good one, there are expressions of poverty hidden in a deep place, such as the tremendous loneliness of people who have been abandoned and who are suffering...

As far as I am concerned, the greatest suffering is to feel alone, unwanted, unloved.

The greatest suffering is also having no one, forgetting what an intimate, truly human relationship is, not knowing what it means to be loved, not having a family or friends. — *O W, 91*

JOY

Joy is not simply a matter of temperament. In the service of God and souls, it is always hard to be joyful — all the more reason why we should try to acquire it and make it grow in our hearts.

Joy is prayer; joy is strength; joy is love; joy is a net of love by which we catch souls. God loves a cheerful giver. She gives most who gives with joy. If in the work you have difficulties and you accept them with joy, with a big smile — in this like in any other thing — they will see your good works and glorify the Father. The best way to show your gratitude is to accept everything with joy. A joyful heart is the normal result of a heart burning with love.

Joy is a need and power for us, even physically. A sister who has cultivated a spirit of joy feels less tired and is always ready to go on doing good. The devil is a carrier of dust and dirt — he uses every chance to throw what he has at us. A joyful heart knows how to protect itself from such dirt: Jesus can take full possession of our soul only if it surrenders itself joyfully. St. Teresa was worried about her sisters only when she saw any of them lose their joy. God is joy. He is love. A sister filled with joy preaches without preaching. A joyful sister is like the sunshine of God's love, the hope of eternal happiness, the flame of burning love.

In our society, a cheerful disposition is one of the main virtues required for a Missionary of Charity. The spirit of our society is total surrender, loving trust, and cheerfulness. That is why the society expects us to accept humiliations readily and with joy; to live the life of poverty with cheerful trust; to imitate the chastity of Mary, the cause of our joy; to offer cheerful obedience from inward joy; to minister to Christ in his distressing disguise with cheerful devotion. — *TS, 46–47*

HOLINESS

Make sure that you let God's grace work in your souls by accepting whatever he gives you, and giving him whatever he takes from you. True holiness consists in doing God's will with a smile. — *GG, 37*

In order to be saints, you have to seriously want to be one.

St. Thomas Aquinas assures us that holiness "is nothing else but a resolution made, the heroic act for a soul that surrenders to God." And he adds: "Spontaneously we love God, we run toward him, we get close to him, we possess him."

Our willingness is important because it changes us into the image of God and likens us to him! The decision to be holy is a very dear one.

Renunciation, temptations, struggles, persecutions, and all kinds of sacrifice are what surround the soul that has opted for holiness.

— OW, 3

Jesus wants us to be holy as his Father is.

Holiness consists of carrying out God's will with joy.

Each one of us is what he is in the eyes of God. We are all called to be saints. There is nothing extraordinary about this call. We all have been created in the image of God to love and to be loved.   — MTR, 146

You may be writing, and the fullness of your heart will come to your hand also. Your heart may speak through writing. Your heart may speak through your eyes also. You know that when you look at people they must be able to see God in your eyes. If you get distracted and worldly then they will not be able to see God like that. The fullness of our heart is expressed in our eyes, in our touch, in what we write, in what we say, in the way we walk, the way we receive, the way we need. That is the fullness of our heart expressing itself in many different ways.

— MTR, 95

We all long for heaven where God is, but we have it in our power to be in heaven with him right now, to be happy with him this moment. But being happy with him now means loving as he loves, helping as he helps, giving as he gives, serving as he serves, rescuing as he rescues — and being with him twenty-four hours a day.   — JWS, 83

SOURCES

Mother Teresa: Essential Writings, ed. Jean Maalouf (Maryknoll, NY: Orbis Books, 2001).

Selections taken from the following sources:

GG   Mother Teresa of Calcutta, *A Gift of God: Prayers and Meditations* (New York: Harper & Row, 1975).

HJ   Mother Teresa, *Heart of Joy: The Transforming Power of Self-Giving,* ed. José Luis González-Balado (Ann Arbor, MI: Servant Books, 1987).

HW   Mother Teresa, *In the Heart of the World: Thoughts, Stories, and Prayers,* ed. Becky Benenate (Novato, CA: New World Library, 1997).

JWS   Mother Teresa, *Jesus the Word to Be Spoken: Prayers and Meditations for Every Day of the Year,* comp. Brother Angelo Devananda (Ann Arbor, MI: Servant Books, 1986).

MTR   *The Mother Teresa Reader: A Life for God,* comp. LaVonne Neff (Ann Arbor, MI: Servant Publications, 1995).

OHFL   Mother Teresa, *One Heart Full of Love,* ed. José Luis González-Balado (Ann Arbor, MI: Servant Books, 1984).

OW   Mother Teresa, *In My Own Words,* comp. José Luis González-Balado (Liguori, MO: Liguori Publications, 1996).

SV   Eileen Egan, *Such a Vision of the Street: Mother Teresa — The Spirit and the Work* (New York: Doubleday, 1986).

TS   Mother Teresa, *Total Surrender,* ed. Brother Angelo Devananda (Ann Arbor, MI: Servant Books, 1985).

THREE

MOHANDAS GANDHI

Great Soul of India

Mohandas K. Gandhi (1869–1948), hero of the Indian independence movement, did more than any person in history to advance the theory and practice of nonviolence. Others had embraced nonviolence as a personal or religious code. But it was Gandhi who demonstrated that the same spirit of nonviolence he embraced as a principle of life could be harnessed as a principle of political struggle. In his life he was often described as a "saint trying to be a politician." Gandhi preferred to say that he was, rather, a politician "trying to be a saint." In any case, for Gandhi the search for God was inseparable from service to the poor and oppressed, and true worship was inseparable from active love.

Though his relevance is universal, Gandhi has always presented a special attraction and challenge for Christians. As a young lawyer in South Africa he was pursued by evangelical friends who avidly sought his conversion. Gandhi read the Bible and attended their services, only to be confirmed in the Hindu faith of his birth. But it was a faith always open to a greater truth, a truth larger, as he perceived it, than the capacity of any person, church, or tradition to contain it completely. Later, as he came to regard the personal search for truth as inseparable from the public struggle for freedom and justice, Gandhi posed a different kind of challenge. Here was a Hindu who politely rejected the dogmatic claims of Christianity while embracing, with every ounce of his will, the ethical claims of Christ.

In either case, Gandhi's influence on Christians has owed less to his specific comments on Christianity than to his ability to recall, in his witness, the features of Christ and the gospel commandment of love. Nevertheless, Gandhi's writings document his profound appreciation

36

for Jesus, the influence of Christian ideals, and his devotion to many Christian friends. His frequent recourse to Christian scripture led spiteful critics to accuse him of being a "secret Christian," a charge Gandhi considered both a libel and a compliment: "a libel because there are men who believe me to be capable of being secretly anything, . . . a compliment in that it is a reluctant acknowledgment of my capacity for appreciating the beauties of Christianity." Indeed, if left with the Sermon on the Mount and his own interpretation of it, he said he would gladly call himself a Christian. But he conceded honestly that his interpretation would fall short of orthodoxy.

Gandhi's difficulties with Christianity were at once theological and ethical. He could not bring himself to regard Jesus Christ as the only Son of God. Nor could he accept that his salvation hinged on such a confession. At the same time, the behavior of Christians left him doubtful that their religion had any superior or unique claim to the truth.

His early childhood impressions of Christianity centered on the belief that Indian converts were required to renounce their cultural heritage, to embrace "beef and brandy." Later experiences in England and South Africa did little to change his opinion. It was his encounter with the writings of Leo Tolstoy that sparked his discovery of what he called the "true message of Jesus," as represented in the Sermon on the Mount, with its emphasis on the "law of love." In Tolstoy Gandhi found a confirmation of his own inclination to distinguish between the message of Jesus and the teachings and practice of the Christian church. Thus, Jesus became for Gandhi an object of reverence and devotion, uncompromised by the failures and betrayals of his Christian followers.

Gandhi returned to India, where he tested and developed his philosophy of nonviolent action in the struggle for Indian independence. In the context of his encounters with Christians Gandhi continued to express his opinions on the subject of Jesus, Christianity, and the missionary enterprise. He confessed his sincere devotion to the figure of Jesus, whom he regarded as an ideal representative of nonviolence. He embraced not only the Sermon on the Mount but Jesus' redemptive suffering unto death, and he cited Jesus' example of loving service as the essence of true religion. At the same time he voiced criticism of orthodox Christianity, both for its dogmatic claims and its ethical shortcomings. Christendom, judging from his experience on the receiving end, appeared to be the very negation of the Sermon on the Mount.

Long before his death at the hands of a young Hindu fanatic on January 30, 1948, Gandhi's authority as the Mahatma, or "Great Soul," had spontaneously extended beyond his native country. Although his particular brand of asceticism conformed to Indian cultural norms, he was one of those examples of unquestioned holiness — St. Francis comes to mind as another — whose challenge transcends the limits of his age and culture. It is the example of someone like Gandhi that makes it impossible for most Christians to maintain the notion that salvation is restricted to the visible church. Indeed, Gandhi is a powerful argument for the capacity of non-Christians to function for Christians as saints — living icons of the invisible God.

This is not to bestow on Gandhi the status of "honorary Christian." He remained a committed Hindu and always resisted, with good humor, the opinion of those Christians who held that "if only he accepted Christ" his example would be complete. Jesus, as Gandhi observed, called human beings not to a new religion but a new life. "If I have read the Bible correctly," he said, "I know many men who have never heard the name of Jesus Christ or have even rejected the official interpretation of Christianity who will, probably, if Jesus came in our midst today in the flesh, be owned by him more than many of us."

There are undoubtedly many Christians who, because of Gandhi, have become better Christians, who have rediscovered different emphases in the gospel, and have been led to view the suffering figure of Christ through new eyes.

RELIGION

I could not be leading a religious life unless I identified myself with the whole of mankind, and that I could not do unless I took part in politics. The whole gamut of man's activities today constitutes an indivisible whole. You cannot divide social, economic, political and purely religious work into watertight compartments. I do not know any religion apart from human activity. It provides a moral basis to all other activities which they would otherwise lack, reducing life to a maze of "sound and fury signifying nothing."   — AMAB, 90

I would say with those who say "God is Love," God is Love. But deep down in me I used to say that though God may be Love, God is Truth above all. If it is possible for the human tongue to give the fullest description of God, I have come to the conclusion that God is Truth. Two years ago I went a step further and said that Truth is God. You will see the fine distinction between the two statements, "God is Truth" and "Truth is God." ... And when you want to find Truth as God, the only inevitable means is love, that is, nonviolence, and since I believe that ultimately the means and ends are convertible terms, I should not hesitate to say that God is love.   —*AMAB*, 91

I do dimly perceive that whilst everything around me is ever changing, ever dying, there is underlying all that change a living power that is changeless, that holds all together, that creates, dissolves, and recreates. That informing power or spirit is God, and since nothing else I see merely through the senses can or will persist, He alone is.

And is this power benevolent or malevolent? I see it as purely benevolent. For I can see that in the midst of death life persists, in the midst of untruth truth persists, in the midst of darkness light persists. Hence I gather that God is Life, Truth, Light. He is Love. He is the Supreme Good.

But He is no God who merely satisfies the intellect, if He ever does. God to be God must rule the heart and transform it. He must express Himself in even the smallest act of His votary. This can only be done through a definite realization more real than the five senses can ever produce. Sense perceptions can be, often are, false and deceptive, however real they may appear to us. Where there is realization outside the senses it is infallible. It is proved not by extraneous evidence but in the transformed conduct and character of those who felt the real presence of God within.

Such testimony is to be found in the experience of an unbroken line of prophets and sages in all countries and climes. To reject this evidence is to deny oneself.

This realization is preceded by an immovable faith. He who would in his own person test the fact of God's presence can do so by a living faith. And since faith itself cannot be proved by extraneous evidence, the safest course is to believe in the moral government of the world and therefore in the supremacy of the moral law, the law of Truth and Love. Exercise of faith will be the safest where there is a clear determination summarily to reject all that is contrary to Truth and Love.

I cannot account for the existence of evil by any rational method. To want to do so is to be coequal with God. I am therefore humble enough to recognize evil as such. And I call God long-suffering and patient precisely because He permits evil in the world. I know that He has no evil. He is the author of it and yet is untouched by it.

I know too that I shall never know God if I do not wrestle with and against evil even at the cost of life itself. I am fortified in the belief by my own humble and limited experience. The purer I try to become the nearer I feel to be to God. How much more should I be, when my faith is not a mere apology as it is today but has become as immovable as the Himalayas and as white and bright as the snows on their peaks? Meanwhile I invite the correspondent to pray with [John Henry] Newman who sang from experience:

> Lead, kindly light, amidst the encircling gloom,
> Lead Thou me on;
> The night is dark and I am far from home,
> Lead Thou me on;
> Keep Thou my feet, I do not ask to see
> The distant scene; one step enough for me.

— GC, 70

To me God is Truth and Love; God is ethics and morality; God is fearlessness. God is the source of Light and Life and yet He is above and beyond all these. God is conscience. He is even the atheism of the atheist. For in His boundless love God permits the atheist to live. He is the searcher of hearts. He transcends speech and reason. He knows us and our hearts better than we do ourselves. He does not take us at our word for He knows that we often do not mean it, some knowingly and others unknowingly. He is a personal God to those who need His personal presence. He is embodied to those who need His touch. He is the purest essence. He simply *is* to those who have faith. He is all things to all men.

— GC, 71

I am not a visionary. I claim to be a practical idealist. The religion of nonviolence is not meant merely for the *rishis* and saints. It is meant for the common people as well. Nonviolence is the law of our species as violence is the law of the brute. The spirit lies dormant in the brute, and he knows no law but that of physical might. The dignity of man requires obedience to a higher law — to the strength of the spirit.

I have therefore ventured to place before India the ancient law of self-sacrifice. For Satyagraha [*Gandhi's term for active nonviolence, or "truth force"*] and its offshoots, noncooperation and civil resistance are nothing but new names for the law of suffering. The *rishis* who discovered the law of nonviolence in the midst of violence were greater geniuses than Newton. They were themselves greater warriors than Wellington. Having themselves known the use of arms, they realized their uselessness, and taught a weary world that its salvation lay not through violence but nonviolence.

Nonviolence in its dynamic condition means conscious suffering. It does not mean meek submission to the will of the evildoer, but it means putting one's whole soul against the will of the tyrant. Working under this law of our being, it is possible for a single individual to defy the whole might of an unjust empire, to save his honor, his religion, and his soul.

— *GC*, 73

I will give you a talisman. Whenever you are in doubt, or when the self becomes too much with you, try the following expedient:

Recall the face of the poorest and the most helpless man whom you may have seen and ask yourself if the step you contemplate is going to be of any use to him. Will he be able to gain anything by it? Will it restore him to a control over his own life and destiny? In other words, will it lead to . . . self-rule for the hungry and also spiritually starved millions of our countrymen?

Then you will find your doubts and yourself melting away. — *GC*, 74

I have found that life persists in the midst of destruction and therefore there must be a higher law than that of destruction. Only under that law would a well-ordered society be intelligible and life worth living. And if that is the law of life, we have to work it out in daily life. Whenever there are jars, whenever you are confronted with an opponent, conquer him with love — in this crude manner I have worked it out in my life. That does not mean that all my difficulties are solved. Only I have found that this law of love has answered as the law of destruction has never done. The more I work at this law, the more I feel delight in life, delight in the scheme of this universe. It gives me a peace and a meaning of the mysteries of nature that I have no power to describe. — *GC*, 74

The only way to find God is to see Him in His creation and be one with it. This can only be done by service of all. I am a part and parcel of the whole, and I cannot find Him apart from the rest of humanity. My countrymen are my nearest neighbors. They have become so helpless, so resourceless, so inert that I must concentrate myself on serving them. If I could persuade myself that I should find Him in a Himalayan cave I would proceed there immediately. But I know that I cannot find Him apart from humanity.   — GC, 74

I believe in the message of truth delivered by all the religious teachers of the world. And it is my constant prayer that I may never have a feeling of anger against my traducers, that even if I fall a victim to an assassin's bullet, I may deliver up my soul with the remembrance of me to be written down an imposter if my lips utter a word of anger or abuse against my assailant at the last moment.   — GC, 74

THE MESSAGE OF JESUS

The message of Jesus, as I understand it, is contained in His Sermon on the Mount unadulterated and taken as a whole, and even in connection with the Sermon on the Mount, my own humble interpretation of the message is in many respects different from the orthodox. The message, to my mind, has suffered distortion in the West. It may be presumptuous for me to say so, but as a devotee of truth, I should not hesitate to say what I feel. I know that the world is not waiting to know my opinion on Christianity.

One's own religion is after all a matter between oneself and one's Maker and no one else's, but if I feel impelled to share my thoughts with you this evening, it is because I want to enlist your sympathy in my search for truth and because so many Christian friends are interested in my thoughts on the teachings of Jesus. If then I had to face only the Sermon on the Mount and my own interpretation of it, I should not hesitate to say, "Oh yes, I am a Christian." But I know that at the present moment if I said any such thing I would lay myself open to the gravest misinterpretation. I should lay myself open to fraudulent claims because I would have then to tell you what my own meaning of Christianity is, and I have no desire myself to give you my own view of Christianity. But negatively I can tell you that, in my humble opinion, much of what passes as Christianity is a negation of the Sermon on the Mount. And please mark my words, I am not at the present moment speaking of the Christian conduct. I am speaking of the Christian belief, of Christianity as it is understood in the West. I am painfully aware of the fact that conduct everywhere falls short of belief. But I don't say this by way of criticisms. I know from the treasures of my own experience that, although I am every moment of my life trying to live up to my professions, my conduct falls short of these professions. Far, therefore, be it from me to say this in a spirit of criticism. But I am placing before you my fundamental difficulties.

When I began as a prayerful student to study the Christian literature in South Africa in 1893, I asked myself "Is this Christianity?" and have always got the Vedic answer, "Neti, Neti" (not this, not this), and the deepest in me tells me that I am right.

I claim to be a man of faith and prayer, and even if I was cut to pieces, God would give me the strength not to deny Him, and to assert that He is. The Muslim says: He is and there is no one else. The Christian says the same thing and so the Hindu, and, if I may say so, even the Buddhist says the same thing, if in different words. We may each of us be putting our own interpretation on the word God — God who embraces not only this tiny globe of ours, but millions and billions of such globes. How can we, little crawling creatures, so utterly helpless as He has made us, how could we possibly measure His greatness, His boundless love, His infinite compassion, such that He allows man insolently to deny Him, wrangle about Him, and cut the throat of his fellow-man? How can we measure the greatness of God who is so forgiving, so divine? Thus, though we may utter the same words they have not the same meaning for us all. And hence I say that we do not need to proselytize through our speech or writing. We can only do it really with our lives. Let them be open books for all to study. Would that I could persuade the missionary friends to take this view of their mission. Then there will be no distrust, no suspicion, no jealously and no dissension.   — *GC*, 20

I shall tell you how, to an outsider like me, the story of Christ, as told in the New Testament, has struck. My acquaintance with the Bible began nearly forty-five years ago, and that was through the New Testament ... When I came to the New Testament and the Sermon on the Mount, I began to understand the Christian teaching, and the teaching of the Sermon on the Mount echoed something I had learnt in childhood and something which seemed to be part of my being and which I felt was being acted up to in the daily life around me ... This teaching was nonretaliation, or nonresistance to evil. Of all the things I read, what remained with me forever was that Jesus came almost to give a new law — though he of course had said he had not come to give a new law, but tack something on to the old Mosaic law. Well, he changed it so that it became a new law — not an eye for an eye, and a tooth for a tooth, but to be ready to receive two blows when only one was given, and to go two miles when they were asked to go one.

I said to myself, this is what one learns in one's childhood. Surely this is not Christianity. For all I had then been given to understand was that to be a Christian was to have a brandy bottle in one hand and beef in the other. The Sermon on the Mount, however, falsified the impression. As my contact with real Christians, i.e., men living in fear of God, increased, I saw that the Sermon on the Mount was the whole of Christianity for him who wanted to live a Christian life. It is that Sermon which has endeared Jesus to me . . .

Reading, therefore, the whole story in that light, it seems to me that Christianity has yet to be lived, unless one says that where there is boundless love and no idea of retaliation whatsoever, it is Christianity that lives. But then it surmounts all boundaries and book teaching. Then it is something indefinable, not capable of being preached to men, not capable of being transmitted from mouth to mouth, but from heart to heart. But Christianity is not commonly understood in that way . . .

As long as it remains a hunger still unsatisfied, as long as Christ is not yet born, we have to look forward to Him. When real peace is established, we will not need demonstrations, but it will be echoed in our life, not only in individual life, but in corporate life. Then we shall say Christ is born.   — GC, 21–23

For many, many years I have regarded Jesus of Nazareth as one amongst the mighty teachers that the world has had, and I say this in all humility. I claim humility for this expression for the simple reason that this is exactly what I feel. Of course, Christians claim a higher place for Jesus of Nazareth than as a non-Christian and as a Hindu I have been able to feel. I purposely use the word "feel" instead of "give," because I consider that neither I, nor anybody else, can possibly arrogate to himself the claim of giving place to a great man . . .

I can say that Jesus occupies in my heart the place of one of the great teachers who have made a considerable influence on my life. Leave the Christians alone for the present. I shall say to the Hindus that your lives will be incomplete unless you reverently study the teachings of Jesus. I have come to the conclusion, in my own experience, that those who, no matter to what faith they belong, reverently study the teaching of other faiths, broaden their own instead of narrowing their hearts. Personally, I do not regard any of the great religions of the world as false. All have served in enriching mankind and are now even serving their purpose.

There is one thing which occurs to me, which came to me in my early studies of the Bible. It seized me immediately I read the passage: "Make this world the Kingdom of God and His righteousness and everything will be added unto you." I tell you that if you will understand, appreciate, and act up to the spirit of this passage, you won't even need to know what place Jesus or any other teacher occupies in your heart. If you will do the proper scavenger's work, clean and purify your hearts and get them ready, you will find that all these mighty teachers take their places with our invitation from us. — *GC,* 23–24

Although I have devoted a large part of my life to the study of religion and to discussion with religious leaders of all faiths, I know very well that I cannot but seem presumptuous in writing about Jesus Christ and trying to explain what He means to me. I do so only because my Christian friends have told me on more than a few occasions that for the very reason that I am not a Christian and that (I shall quote their words exactly) "I do not accept Christ in the bottom of my heart as the only Son of God," it is impossible for me to understand the profound significance of His teachings, or to know and interpret the greatest source of spiritual strength that man has ever known.

Although this may or may not be true in my case, I have reasons to believe that it is an erroneous point of view. I believe that such an estimate is incompatible with the message that Jesus Christ gave to the world. For He was, certainly, the highest example of One who wished to give everything, asking nothing in return, and not caring what creed might happen to be professed by the recipient. I am sure that if He were living here now among men, He would bless the lives of many who perhaps have never even heard His name, if only their lives embodied the virtues of which He was a living example on earth; the virtues of loving one's neighbor as oneself and of doing good and charitable works among one's fellow men.

What, then, does Jesus mean to me? To me, He was one of the greatest teachers humanity has ever had. To His believers, He was God's only begotten son. Could the fact that I do or do not accept this belief make

Jesus have any more or less influence in my life? Is all the grandeur of His teaching and of His doctrine to be forbidden to me? I cannot believe so. To me it implies a spiritual birth. My interpretation, in other words, is that in Jesus' own life is the key of His nearness to God; that He expressed as no other could, the spirit and will of God. It is in this sense that I see Him and recognize Him as the son of God. But I do believe that something of this spirit that Jesus exemplified in the highest measure, in its most profound human sense, does exist. I must believe this; if I did not believe I should be a skeptic; and to be a skeptic is to live a life that is empty and lacks moral content. Or, what is the same thing, to condemn the entire human race to a negative end.

It is true that there certainly is reason for skepticism when one observes the bloody butchery that European aggressors have unloosed, and when one thinks about the misery and suffering prevalent in every corner of the world, as well as the pestilence and famine that always follow, terribly and inevitably, upon war. In the face of this, how can one speak seriously of the divine spirit incarnate in man? Because these acts of terror and murder offend the conscience of man; because man knows that they represent evil; because in the inner depths of his heart and of his mind, he deplores them. And because, moreover, when he does not go astray, misled by false teachings or corrupted by false leaders, man has within his breast an impulse for good and compassion that is the spark of divinity, and which some day, I believe, will burst forth into the full flower that is the hope of all mankind. An example of this flowering may be found in the figure and in the life of Jesus. I refuse to believe that there now exists or has ever existed a person that has not made use of His example to lesson his sins, even though he may have done so without realizing it. The lives of all have, in some greater or lesser degree, been changed by His presence, His actions, and the words spoken by His divine voice.

I believe that it is impossible to estimate the merits of the various religions of the world, and moreover I believe that it is unnecessary and harmful even to attempt it. But each one of them, in my judgment, embodies a common motivating force: the desire to uplift man's life and give it purpose. And because the life of Jesus has the significance and the transcendency to which I have alluded I believe that He belongs not solely to Christianity, but to the entire world; to all races and people, it matters little under what flag, name, or doctrine they may work, profess a faith, or worship a God inherited from their ancestors.   —*GC,* 27–28

Jesus was the most active resister known perhaps to history. His was nonviolence par excellence. —*MG, 79*

Religion without compassion is a fraud. Compassion is at the very root of religion, and one who forsakes it, forsakes God. One who forsakes the poor forsakes everything. If we do not look after the poor and the untouchables, we are sure to perish. —*MG, 81*

My experience tells me that the Kingdom of God is within us, and that we can realize it not by saying, "Lord, Lord," but by doing God's will and God's work. If therefore we wait for the Kingdom to come as something coming from outside, we shall be sadly mistaken. Do you know that there are thousands of villages where people are starving and which are on the brink of ruin? If we would listen to the voice of God, I assure you we would hear God say that we are taking God's name in vain if we do not think of the poor and help them. If you cannot render the help that they need, it is no use talking of service of God and service of the poor. Try to identify yourselves with the poor by actually helping them.

—*MG, 81*

NONVIOLENCE

Just as one must learn the art of killing in the training for violence, so one must learn the art of dying in the training for nonviolence. Violence does not mean emancipation from fear, but discovering the means of combating the cause of fear. Nonviolence on the other hand has no cause for fear. The votary of nonviolence has to cultivate the capacity for sacrifice of the highest type in order to be free from fear. The votary of nonviolence has only one fear, that is of God. —*AMAB, 77–78*

It is no nonviolence if we merely love those who love us. It is nonviolence only when we love those who hate us. I know how difficult it is to follow this grand law of love. But are not all great and good things difficult to do? Love of the hater is the most difficult of all. But by the grace of God even the most difficult thing becomes easy to accomplish if we want to do it. —*MG, 97–98*

The basic principle on which the practice of nonviolence rests is that what holds good in respect of yourself, holds good equally in respect of the whole universe. All humans in essence are alike. What is, therefore, possible for me is possible for everybody. Pursuing further this line of reasoning, I came to the conclusion that if I could find a nonviolent solution of the various problems that arise in one particular village, the lesson learned from it would enable me to tackle in a nonviolent manner all similar problems in India.

In its positive form, nonviolence means the largest love, the greatest charity. If I am a follower of nonviolence, I must love my enemy. I must apply the same rules to the wrong-doer who is my enemy or a stranger to me, as I would to my wrong-doing father or son. This active nonviolence necessarily includes truth and fearlessness. The practice of nonviolence calls forth the greatest courage.   — MG, 98

The goal ever recedes from us. The greater the progress, the greater the recognition of our unworthiness. Satisfaction lies in the effort, not in the attainment. Full effort is full victory. Therefore, though I realize more than ever how far I am from that goal, for me the law of complete Love is the law of my being. Each time I fail, my effort shall be all the more determined for my failure.   — MG, 102

PRAYER

I believe that prayer is the very soul and essence of religion, and therefore prayer must be the very core of the life of humanity, for no one can live without religion. There are some who in the egotism of their reason declare that they have nothing to do with religion. But it is like a person saying that he breathes but that he has no nose. Whether by reason, or by instinct, or by superstition, humanity acknowledges some sort of relationship with the divine.

Prayer is the very core of life. Prayer is either petitional or in its wider sense is inward communion. In either case, the ultimate result is the same. Even when it is petitional, the petition should be for the cleansing and purification of the soul, for freeing it from the layers of ignorance and darkness that envelope it. The one who hungers for the awakening of the divine within must fall back on prayer. But prayer is no mere exercise of words or of the ears; it is no mere repetition of empty formulas. Any amount of repetition of God's name is futile if it fails to stir the soul. It is better in prayer to have a heart without words than words without a heart. It must be in a clear response to the spirit which hungers for it, and even as a hungry person relishes a hearty meal, a hungry soul will relish a heart-felt prayer. Without prayer there is no inner peace.

We are born to serve our fellow men and women, and we cannot properly do so unless we are wide awake. There is an eternal struggle raging in humanity's breast between the powers of darkness and of light, and the one who has not the anchor of prayer to rely upon will be victim to the powers of darkness. Persons of prayer will be at peace with themselves and with the whole world. Those who go about the affairs of the world without a prayerful heart will be miserable and will make the world also miserable. Apart therefore from its bearing on humanity's condition after death, prayer has incalculable value for humanity in this world of the living. Prayer is the only means of bringing orderliness and peace and repose in our daily acts.

Begin therefore your day with prayer, and make it so soulful that it may remain with you until the evening. Close the day with prayer so that you may have a peaceful night free from dreams and nightmares. Do not worry about the form of prayer. Let it be any form; it should be such as can put us into communion with the divine. Only, whatever be the form, let not the spirit wander while the words of prayer run on out of your mouth.

You whose mission in life is service of your fellow men and women will go to pieces if you do not impose on yourselves some sort of discipline, and prayer is a necessary spiritual discipline. It is discipline and restraint that separates us from the brute. If we want to be men and women walking with our heads erect and not walking on all fours, let us understand and put ourselves under voluntary discipline and restraint.

—*MG*, 129–31

There is really only one prayer that we may offer: "Thy will be done." Someone will ask where is the sense in offering such a prayer. The answer is: Prayer should not be understood in a gross sense. We are aware of the presence of God in our heart, and in order to shake off attachment, we for the moment think of God as different from ourselves and pray to God. That is to say, we do not wish to go where our wayward will may lead us but where the Lord takes us. We do not know whether it is good to live or die. Therefore we should not take delight in living, nor should we tremble at the thought of death. We should be equally minded toward both. This is the ideal. It may be long before we reach it, and only a few of us can attain it. Even then we must keep it constantly in

view, and the more difficult it seems of attainment, the greater should be
the effort we put forth.   —MG, 131–32

Prayer is not to be performed with the lips, but with the heart. And that
is why it can be performed equally by the dumb and the stammerer, by
the ignorant and the stupid. And the prayers of those whose tongues are
nectared but whose hearts are full of poison are never heard. Those who
would pray to God must cleanse their hearts. It is faith that steers us
through stormy seas, faith that moves mountains, and faith that jumps
across the ocean. That faith is nothing but a living, wide-awake consciousness of God within. The one who has achieved that faith wants
nothing. Bodily diseased he is spiritually healthy, physically pure, he rolls
in spiritual riches.

   The language of the lips is easily taught; but who can teach the language of the heart? Only the true devotee knows it and can teach it. I
have therefore suggested the religion of service as the means. God seeks
for God's seat the heart of the one who serves humanity. A prayerful
heart is the vehicle and service makes the heart prayerful.   —MG, 133

SOURCES

AMAB   *All Men Are Brothers: Life and Thoughts of Mahatma*
         Gandhi, ed. Krishna Kripalani (Ahmedabad: Navajivan,
         1960).

GC   *Gandhi on Christianity,* ed. Robert Ellsberg (Maryknoll,
         NY: Orbis Books, 1991).

MG   *Mohandas Gandhi: Essential Writings,* ed. John Dear
         (Maryknoll, NY: Orbis Books, 2002).

FOUR

MADELEINE DELBRÊL

Missionary without a Boat

Madeleine Delbrêl (1904–1964) grew up in a working-class family in southern France. Slight (only four and a half feet tall) and nimble, she exuded an energy and passion for life that enlivened her every surrounding. Above all she had a passion for the absolute. Though she spent her youth as a confirmed atheist, from the time — when she was twenty-four — that she became convinced of God's existence, she saw no alternative but to dedicate her life to his service. Her conversion was an overwhelming, "bedazzling" experience that marked her forever.

Delbrêl briefly considered becoming a nun, but she ultimately discerned that her vocation was in the world. God might call some people to stand apart, she decided, but "there are those he leaves among the crowds... These are the people who have an ordinary job, an ordinary household, or an ordinary celibacy. People with ordinary sicknesses and ordinary times of grieving... These are the people of ordinary life, the people we might meet on any street." Casting her lot with this anonymous crowd, she declared, "We, the ordinary people of the streets, believe with all our might that this street, this world, where God has placed us, is our place of holiness."

With several friends she conceived the idea of a small lay community dedicated to leading a contemplative Christian life in the midst of the world. For the sake of this vocation she prepared herself for three years with ardent discipline, quietly praying, studying scripture, and taking courses in social work. Finally, in 1933, with the blessing of her spiritual director, she and her companions set forth for Ivry, a working-class city near Paris that was a stronghold of the French Communist Party.

From the start, the local pastor had trouble comprehending what these women were up to. Having expected that they would occupy themselves with parish duties, he was perplexed when they seemed more interested in spending time with their Communist neighbors. Delbrêl and her companions were themselves struggling to find their way. In their engagement with the workers, who had been long estranged from the church, they felt they were undertaking a new kind of missionary work. They called themselves "missionaries without a boat" — not traveling overseas, but crossing the borders of faith to bear witness to the gospel in friendship and solidarity.

Over time they won their neighbors' trust. With the outbreak of World War II the city government even asked Delbrêl to oversee services for refugees flooding the town. She organized soup kitchens, clothing drives, and emergency shelters. In recognition of this service, the Communist government wanted to give her a medal after the war, but she declined the honor.

In the meantime, wartime sufferings had broken down many of the historic barriers between the church and the working class, while revealing how much work remained to be done. Cardinal Suhard of Paris endorsed the view that historically Catholic France was now a "mission territory." Calling for a Mission de France, he established a seminary to train priests to work in factories alongside the poor. Delbrêl was invited to serve as a lay advisor. It was the beginning of what became the Worker Priest movement.

Delbrêl threw herself into this movement with all her vitality and enthusiasm. But the movement was short-lived. Conservative sectors of the church in France and Rome opposed this "compromise" with the secular world — particularly the strongly Marxist atmosphere of the trade unions. The experiment was eventually suppressed by the Vatican.

Delbrêl remained as committed as ever to her essential missionary project — building a bridge between the church and the secular world. Apart from any other accomplishment, such contact with unbelievers strengthened her own faith, forcing her, as she said, to be more authentic, to think critically, to avoid pious clichés. When asked how she prayed, she described her "Prayer of the Agenda." It was simply a heightened awareness of the presence of God in all the ordinary activities of life — whether meeting people, answering the phone, or running errands. In these ordinary circumstances, she insisted, a person could experience the deepest spiritual dimensions of life.

At last, with the arrival of Pope John XXIII ("a tiny miracle of God," she called him) she lived to see the beginning of a new season in the church. In many ways Delbrêl's spirit was embraced by the Second Vatican Council, especially in its affirmation of the special vocation of the laity. As Delbrêl put it, "We are called to be the visible body of Christ in the midst of the human body of society." In turn, she certainly would have embraced the opening words of Gaudium et Spes, the final document of the Council, which she did not live to see: "The joy and hope, the grief and anguish, of the people of our time, especially of those who are poor or afflicted in any way, are the joy and hope, the grief and anguish of the followers of Christ as well."

But Delbrêl did not place her hopes in grand and historic events. The most significant events in the universe, she believed, were often small and seemingly ordinary: "Each tiny act is an extraordinary event, in which heaven is given to us, in which we are able to give heaven to others... Is someone asking us to do anything? Here you are! It's God coming to love us. Is it time to sit down for lunch? Let's go — it's God coming to love us. Let's let him."

The end came for Madeleine Delbrêl as she worked at her desk. She died on October 13, 1964, two weeks before her sixtieth birthday.

WE, THE ORDINARY PEOPLE OF THE STREETS

There are many places where the Spirit blows,
But there is one Spirit that blows in all places.

There are some people whom God takes and sets apart.

There are others he leaves among the crowds, people he does not "withdraw from the world."

These are the people who have an ordinary job, an ordinary household, or an ordinary celibacy. People with ordinary sicknesses, and ordinary times of grieving. People with an ordinary house, and ordinary clothes. These are the people of ordinary life. The people we might meet on any street.

They love the door that opens onto the street, just as their brothers who are hidden from the world love the door that shuts behind them forever.

We, the ordinary people of the streets, believe with all our might that this street, this world, where God has placed us, is our place of holiness.

We believe that we lack nothing here that we need. If we needed something else, God would already have given it to us.

Silence

We do not need to find silence; we already have it. The day we lack silence is the day we have not learned how to keep it.

All the noises around us cause much less disturbance than we ourselves do.

The real noise is the echo things make within us. It is not necessarily talking that breaks the silence. Silence is the place where the Word of God dwells; if we limit ourselves to repeating this word, then we can speak without ceasing to be silent.

Monasteries appear to be the place of praise and the place of the silence that praise requires.

In the street, crushed by the crowd, we make our souls into so many caves of silence wherein the Word of God can dwell and resound.

In those crowds marked by the sins of hatred, lust, and drunkenness, we find a desert of silence, and we recollect ourselves here with great ease, so that God can ring out his name: *"Vox clamans in deserto."*

Solitude

We, the ordinary people of the streets, do not see solitude as the absence of the world but as the presence of God.

Encountering him in all places is what creates our solitude.

For us, being truly alone means participating in God's solitude.

God is so great that nothing can find room anywhere else but within him.

For us, the whole world is like a face-to-face room anywhere else but within him.

We encounter his living causality right there on the busy street corners.

We encounter his imprint on the earth.

We encounter his Providence in the laws of science.

We encounter Christ in all these "little ones" who are his own: the ones who suffer in body, the ones who are bored, the ones who are troubled, the ones who are in need.

We encounter Christ rejected, in the sin that wears a thousand faces.

How could we possibly have the heart to mock these people or to hate them, this multitude of sinners with whom we rub shoulders?

The solitude of God in fraternal charity; it is Christ serving Christ, Christ in the one who is serving and Christ in the one being served.

How could apostolate be a waste of energy or a distraction?

Obedience

We, the ordinary people of the streets, know very well that as long as our own will is alive, we will not be able to love Christ definitively.

We know that only obedience can root us in his death.

We would envy our religious brothers and sisters if we too could not "die to ourselves" a little more each day.

However, for us the tiny circumstances of life are faithful "superiors." They do not leave us alone for a moment; and the "yeses" we have to say to them follow continuously, one after the other.

When we surrender to them without resistance we find ourselves wonderfully liberated from ourselves. We float in Providence like a cork in the ocean waters.

But let's not act like heroes: God trusts nothing to chance; the rhythms of our life are vast because he has willed it so.

From the moment we wake up these circumstances take hold of us. It is the telephone that rings; it is the key that won't work, the bus that doesn't arrive or arrives full, or doesn't wait for us. It is the person sitting next to us who takes up the whole seat; or the vibration of the loose window pane that drives us crazy.

It's the daily routine, one chore that leads to another, some job we wouldn't have chosen. It's the weather and its changes — which is exquisite precisely because it is completely untainted by human doing. It's being cold, or being hot; it's the headache or the toothache. It's the people we meet and the conversations they choose to start. It's the rude man who nearly knocks us off the sidewalk. It's the people who need to kill some time, and so they corner us.

For us, the ordinary people of the streets, obedience means bending to the ways of our times whenever they are not harmful. It means wearing the same clothes as everyone else, taking on the same routines as everyone else, and speaking the same language as everyone else.

When we live with others, obedience also means we set aside our own tastes and leave things in the place others have put them. In this way life becomes an epic film in slow motion. It does not make our head spin. It doesn't take our breath away. Little by little, thread by thread, it eats away at the old man's frame, which cannot be mended and must be made new from the ground up. When we thus become accustomed to giving up our will to so many tiny things, we will no longer find it hard, when the occasion presents itself, to do the will of our boss, our husband, or our parents.

And our hope is that death, too, will be easy. It will not be a big ordeal, but rather the outcome of small ordinary sufferings, to which we have given our assent as they passed, one after the other.

Love

We, the ordinary people of the streets, are certain we can love God as much as he might desire to be loved by us.

We don't regard love as something extraordinary, but as something that consumes. We believe that doing little things for God is as much a way of loving him as doing great deeds. Besides, we're not very well informed about the greatness of our acts. There are nevertheless two things we know for sure: first, whatever we do can't help but be small; and second, whatever God does is great.

And so we go about our activities with a sense of great peace.

We know that all our work consists in not shifting about under grace; in not choosing what we would do; and that it is God who acts through us.

There is nothing difficult for God; the one who grows anxious at difficulties is the one who counts on his own capacity for action.

Because we find that love is work enough for us, we don't take the time to categorize what we are doing as either "contemplation" or "action."

We find that prayer is action and that action is prayer. It seems to us that truly loving action is filled with light.

It seems to us that a soul standing before such action is like a night that is full of expectation for the coming dawn. And when the light breaks, when God's will is clearly understood, she lives it out gently, with poise, peacefully watching her God inspiring her and at work within her. It seems to us that action is also an imploring prayer. It does not at all seem to us that action nails us down to our field of work, our apostolate, or our life.

Quite the contrary, we believe that an action perfectly carried out at the time and place it is required of us binds us to the whole Church, sends us out throughout her body, making us *disponible* in her.

Our feet march upon a street, but our heartbeat reverberates through the whole world. That is why our small acts, which we can't decide whether they're action or contemplation, perfectly join together the love of God and the love of our neighbor.

Giving ourselves over to his will at the same time gives us over to the Church, whom the same will continuously makes our saving mother of grace.

Each docile act makes us receive God totally and give God totally, in a great freedom of spirit.

And thus life becomes a celebration.

Each tiny act is an extraordinary event, in which heaven is given to us, in which we are able to give heaven to others.

It makes no difference what we do, whether we take in hand a broom or a pen. Whether we speak or keep silent. Whether we are sewing or holding a meeting, caring for a sick person or tapping away at the typewriter.

Whatever it is, it's just the outer shell of an amazing inner reality, the soul's encounter, renewed at each moment, in which, at each moment, the soul grows in grace and becomes ever more beautiful for her God.

It is the doorbell ringing? Quick, open the door! It's God coming to love us. Is someone asking us to do something? Here you are!...It's God coming to love us. Is it time to sit down for lunch? Let's go — it's God coming to love us.

Let's let him.   — We, 54–58

MISSIONARIES WITHOUT A BOAT

There has been a lot said about "the desert of love." Love seeks the desert because the desert is where man is handed over to God, stripped bare of his country, his friends, his fields, his home. In the desert a person neither possesses what he loves, nor is he possessed by those who love him; he is totally submitted to God in an immense and intimate encounter.

That is why in every age the Holy Spirit has compelled all lovers to seek the desert.

We, missionaries without a boat, are seized by the same love and led by the same Spirit into new deserts.

From a sand dune, dressed in white, the missionary overlooks an expanse of lands filled with unbaptized peoples. From the top of a long subway staircase, dressed in an ordinary suit or raincoat, we overlook, on each step, during this busy rush-hour time, an expanse of heads, of bustling heads, waiting for the door to open. Caps, berets, hats, and hair of every color. Hundreds of heads — hundreds of souls. And there we stand, above.

And above us, and everywhere, is God.

God is everywhere — and how many souls even take notice?

In a moment, when the subway doors open, we'll climb aboard. We'll see faces, foreheads, eyes, and mouths. Mouths of lonely people in their nature state: some greedy, some impure, some malicious; some mouths that hunger, some filled with every earthly sustenance, but few — very few — that bear the form of the Gospel...

We cannot help wonder how little light there would be if a light shined only for each person in prayer.

Yes, we have our deserts — and love leads us into them.

The same Spirit that leads our white-robed brothers and sisters into their deserts, also leads our beating heart down the turbulent stairways, into the subways, and up again to the darkened streets.

We do not envy our religious brothers and sisters.

In this crowd, heart against heart, crushed between so many bodies, on the seat we share with these three strangers, in the darkened street, our heart beats like a fist closed upon a bird.

The Holy Spirit, the whole Holy Spirit in our tiny heart, a love great as God is beating within us, like a moiling sea struggling to break out, to spread out, to penetrate into all these closed up creatures, into all these impermeable souls.

To be able to pace every street, to sit in every metro, climb up every staircase, carry the Lord God to all places: we are certain to find a soul here or there that has preserved her human fragility before the grace of God, a soul that has forgotten to armor herself in gold or concrete.

And we can pray, pray just as they pray in all the other deserts, pray for all these people so close to us, so close to God.

A desert of people. We can plunge into the crowd as if plunging into the white desert sands...

Lord, Lord, let the thick skin that covers me not be a hindrance to you. Pass through it.

My eyes, my hands, my mouth are yours.

This sad lady in front of me: here is my mouth for you to smile at her.

The child so pale he's almost gray: here are my eyes for you to gaze at him.

The man so tired, so weary: here is my body so that you may give him my seat, here is my voice so that you may say softly to him, "Please sit down."

This smug young man, so dull, so hard: here is my heart, that you may love him, more strongly than he has ever been loved before.

Missions to the desert, unfailing missions, sure missions, missions in which we sow God in the midst of the world, certain that, somewhere, he will take root, for: "There where love is lacking, put love and you will reap love."

The Word of God is not brought to the ends of the world in a suitcase. We carry it in ourselves...

We cannot be missionaries if we have not sincerely, generously, and warmly welcomed the Word of God the Gospel, within ourselves.

The vital dynamic of this word is to take on flesh, to become flesh in us.

And then this word comes to dwell within us, we become capable of being missionaries...

If the missionary priest is the spokesman of God's Word, we missionaries without holy orders, are a sort of sacrament of God's Word.

Once we have heard God's Word, we no longer have the right not to accept it; once we have accepted it, we no longer have the right not to let it become flesh in us; once it has become flesh in us, we no longer have the right to keep it for ourselves alone. Henceforward, we belong to all those who are waiting for the Word.

The time of martyrs come and goes, but the times of witnesses continues without end — and being witnesses means being martyrs.

The incarnation of God's Word in us, this allowing ourselves to be molded by it, is what we call witnessing.

To take the Word of God seriously, we need all the strength of the Holy Spirit.

If our witness is often mediocre, it is because we have not realized that the same kind of heroism is needed to be a witness as to be a martyr.

Charles de Foucauld said, "I must live today as if tonight I were going to die as a martyr."

At the beginning of each hour of the long day, we could say, "I must begin this hour as if I were going to be a martyr, and a witness" — because there is not one second that we have the right to let God's Word lie dormant in us. And this entails awakening a fervor in our very being in the presence of the grace of each moment, a wildly passionate expectation for that strength, without which we would turn traitor.

— We, 59–62

SOLITUDE

Allowing the Gospel message into our life means letting our life become, in the broad and real sense of the word, a religious life, a life referred to, bound back to, God.

The basic revelation of the Gospel is the overwhelming, penetrating presence of God. It is a call to encounter God, and God allows himself to be encountered in solitude...

True solitude is not the absence of people, but the presence of God.

To place our lives before the face of God, to surrender our lives to the movements of God, is to roam free in a space in which we have been given solitude...

Like a person leaving Paris for the desert, and smiling at it from a solitary distance; like a traveler waiting with deep sighs for long days spent at sea; like a monk whose eyes caress the walls of his monastery, let us open our souls to the small solitudes of the day, from the first moment we wake up in the morning.

For our tiny solitude are as immense, as exultant, as holy, as all the world's deserts, because they are filled with the same God, the God who makes solitude holy... The solitude of the few moments crouching to light the stove; the solitude of the kitchen, spent before the tub of beans. The solitude on our knees scrubbing the floor... The brief solitude of going up and down the stairs, a hundred times a day. The solitude of the long hours with the laundry, washing, mending, and ironing...

Because a new connection with solitudes stands apart from us by the distance of the breadth of the door or the space of a quarter hour, we do not grant its eternal value, we do not take it seriously, we do not enter it like a fascinating countryside that stands constantly ready with essential revelations.

The reason the wells of solitude scattered throughout our day do not give us the living water overflowing in them is that our hearts lack expectation.

We cling to time superstitiously.

Though our love may require time, hours are nothing to the love of God, and a willing soul can be overwhelmed by him in a mere instant.

"I will lead you into solitude and there I will speak to your heart."

If our solitudes are for us poor transmitters of the Word, it is because our heart is absent.

There is no solitude without silence. Silence can sometimes mean talking, but silence always means listening. — *We*, 66, 67–68

SILENCE

Why should the wind through the pines, the sand storm, and the squall upon the sea, all count as silence, and not the pounding of the factory machines, the rumbling of the trains at the station, and the clamor of the engines at the intersection?

In each case, it is just the humming of the great laws of the world around us at play.

Why should the song of the lark in the wheat fields, the buzzing of the insects in the night, and the droning of the bees among the thyme, nourish our silence, and not the crowds in the street, the voices of the women in the market, the yells of the men at work, the laughter of the children in the garden, and the songs coming from the bars? All of these are the noises of creatures advancing toward their destiny, all of this is the echo of the house of God in order or in shambles, all of this is the sign of life encountering our life.

Silence does not mean running away, but rather recollecting ourselves in the open space of God.

Silence is not a tiny grass snake that darts off at the slightest noise; it is an eagle with mighty wings that can soar above the commotion of the earth, of the people, of the wind. — *We*, 69

GOODNESS

We have come to realize what dry bread justice is when it is not preceded by or completed with goodness. When public funds are distributed on the occasion of an accident, when they come to provide assistance with the burdens of having children, when they accompany old age, these subsidies, pensions, grants, and benefits correspond to a sort of justice — and moreover increase the already great differences between the rich and the massive poor countries — but they do not in any way substitute for goodness. In such cases, it is not James or John himself who, in his misfortune or well being, finds help; instead, it is a condition or situation that is helped. General measures regulate collective categories. I resist criticizing the justice that society is able to achieve; criticism serves better to provoke progress in what remains to be achieved. What I am trying to say is that goodness is something else; it achieves something else.

For a person to encounter the goodness of Christ in another person is in particular to encounter himself for what he really is...

The goodness of Christ...teaches us that this "who we are," which has been so manhandled by the world, possesses a value that is absolutely independent of wealth, power, smarts, influence, strength, and success. The goodness of Christ works with us; even more, it hopes for something from us, from each one of us. The goodness of Christ is above all something else: an encounter which affirms for us that we exist, which makes us present to ourselves, which walks alongside us in a common life...

This brings us to an example...

I was in a big foreign city many years ago, coming to the last few hours of the several days I had spent there. I was almost entirely out of money, completely exhausted, and was suffering the pain that shakes the animal in the rational animal that we are: the pain of loss brought by death, by the several deaths of those who were of the same flesh as mine. I do not believe that I represented any social category. The clothes I was wearing had nothing particular about them.

I had been walking through the streets for several hours while I waited for my train. And why not say it? I was crying. But I didn't care anymore, and I waited for it to pass. A foreigner. A stranger. A sorrow that all people know, one that brings tears just as certain forms of work bring sweat.

It started to rain; I was hungry. The few coins remaining to me determined what I was permitted to eat. I went into a tiny café that also served food and ordered what I could afford: some raw vegetables. I ate them slowly so that they would be more nourishing and also to give the rain a chance to stop. Every once in a while my eyes filled up with tears. Then, all of a sudden, a warm and comforting arm took me by the shoulders. A voice said to me: "You, coffee. Me, give." It was absolutely clear. I don't remember exactly what happened afterward, which is lucky for me because I don't much care for melodramatic scenes.

I have often spoken about this woman, thought about her, and prayed for her with an inexhaustible gratitude. When I look today for an example of goodness in flesh and bones, she is the one who comes to mind.

What makes this woman a Christian sign, a distant but faithful image of the goodness of God, is that she was good because goodness dwelled within her, and not because I was "one of her own," familially, socially, politically, nationally, or religiously. I was a "stranger" without any identifying marks. I was in need of goodness, and even that goodness that goes by the name of mercy. It was given me by that woman. Today she represents an absolute example of goodness because I was just "anybody," it didn't matter what or who I was, and because what she did for me she did simply because there was goodness in her. In her simple gesture, I discovered everything that goodness has to be in order to be goodness. — *We*, 141–43

Words found after her death

You were alive and I was completely unaware of it. You had fashioned my heart to your size, you had made my life to last as long as you and because you were absent, the whole world seemed to me tiny and ridiculous and the destiny of man stupid and cruel. When I realized that you were living, I thanked you for having given me life, I thanked you for the life of the whole world. — *We*, xi

SOURCE

We   Madeleine Delbrêl, *We, the Ordinary People of the Streets,* trans. David Louis Schindler, Jr., and Charles F. Mann (Grand Rapids, MI: William B. Eerdmans Publishing, 2000).

FIVE

OSCAR ROMERO

Voice of the Voiceless

☐〽〽〽〽〽〽☐

The selection in 1977 of Oscar Romero (1917–80) as archbishop of San Salvador delighted the country's oligarchy as much as it disappointed the activist clergy of the archdiocese. Known as a pious and relatively conservative bishop, there was nothing in his background to suggest that he was a man to challenge the status quo. No one could have predicted that in three short years he would be renowned as the outstanding embodiment of the prophetic church, a "voice for the voiceless," or, as one theologian called him, "a gospel for El Salvador." Nor could one foresee that he would be denounced by his fellow bishops, earn the hatred of the rich and powerful of El Salvador and generate such enmity that he would be targeted for assassination — the first bishop slain at the altar since Thomas Becket in the twelfth century.

Something changed him. Within weeks of his consecration he found himself officiating at the funeral of his friend Rutilio Grande, a Jesuit priest of the archdiocese, who was assassinated as a result of his commitment to social justice. Romero was deeply shaken by this event, which marked a new level in the frenzy of violence overtaking the country. In the weeks and months following Grande's death Romero underwent a profound transformation. Some would speak of a conversion — as astonishing to his new friends as it was to his foes. From a once timid and conventional cleric, there emerged a fearless and outspoken champion of justice. His weekly sermons, broadcast by radio throughout the country, featured an inventory of the week's violations of human rights, casting the glaring light of the gospel on the realities of the day. His increasingly public role as the conscience of the nation earned him not only the bitter enmity of the country's oligarchy, but also the resentment of many of his conservative fellow bishops. There were those among them who muttered that Romero was talking like a subversive.

The church in El Salvador was not the first church to suffer persecution. The anomaly was that here the persecutors dared to call themselves Christians. Their victims did not die simply for clinging to the faith, but for clinging, like Jesus, to the poor. It was this insight that marked a new theological depth in Romero's message. For Romero, the church's option for the poor was not just a matter of pastoral priorities. It was a defining characteristic of Christian faith: "A church that does not unite itself to the poor in order to denounce from the place of the poor the injustice committed against them is not truly the Church of Jesus Christ," he wrote. On another occasion he said, "On this point there is no possible neutrality. We either serve the life of Salvadorans or we are accomplices in their death ... We either believe in a God of life or we serve the idols of death."

Once his course was set, Romero followed his path with courageous consistency. Privately he acknowledged his fears and loneliness, especially the pain he felt from the opposition of his fellow bishops and the apparent distrust of Rome. Consistently he was accused of subordinating the gospel to politics. At the same time he seemed to draw strength and courage from the poor campesinos, who embraced him with affection and understanding. "With this people," he said, "it is not hard to be a good shepherd."

The social contradictions in El Salvador were rapidly reaching the explosion point. Coups, countercoups, and fraudulent elections brought forth a succession of governments, each promising reform, while leaving the military and the death squads free to suppress the people's demand for justice. As avenues for peaceful change were systematically thwarted, full-scale civil war became inevitable. In 1980, weeks before his death, Romero sent a letter to President Jimmy Carter, appealing for a halt to further U.S. military assistance to the junta, "thus avoiding a greater bloodshed in this suffering country." On March 23, 1980, the day before his death, he appealed directly to members of the military, calling on them to refuse illegal orders: "In the name of God, in the name of our tormented people whose cries rise up to heaven, I beseech you, I beg you, I command you, stop the repression."

The next day, as he was saying Mass, a single shot was fired from the rear of the chapel. Romero was struck in the heart and died within minutes.

Romero was immediately acclaimed by the people of El Salvador, and indeed by the poor throughout Latin America, as a true martyr and saint. For Romero, who clearly anticipated his fate, there was never any doubt as to the meaning of such a death. In an interview two weeks before his assassination, he said: "I have frequently been threatened with death. I must say that, as a Christian, I do not believe in death but in the resurrection. If they kill me, I shall rise again in the Salvadoran people."

WORD AND WITNESS

Not just purgatory but hell awaits those who could have done good and did not do it. It is the reverse of the Beatitude that the Bible has for those who are saved, for the saints, "who could have done wrong and did not." Of those who are condemned it will be said: They could have done good and did not.   —July 16, 1977, VL, 4

How I would like to engrave this great idea on each one's heart: Christianity is not a collection of truths to be believed, of laws to be obeyed, of prohibitions. That makes it very distasteful. Christianity is a person, one who loved us so much, one who calls for our love. Christianity is Christ.   —November 6, 1977, VL, 8–9

Do you want to know if your Christianity is genuine? Here is the touchstone: Who do you get along with? Who are those who criticize you? Who are those who do not accept you? Who are those who flatter you? Know from what Christ said once, "I have come not to bring peace, but division." There will be division even in the same family, because some want to live more comfortably by the world's principles, those of power and money. But others have embraced the call of Christ and must reject all that cannot be just in the world.   —November 13, 1977, VL, 9

How beautiful will be the day when all the baptized understand that their work, their job, is a priestly work, that just as I celebrate Mass at this altar, so each carpenter celebrates Mass at his workbench, and each metalworker, each professional, each doctor with the scalpel, the market woman at her stand, is performing a priestly office! How many cabdrivers, I know, listen to this message there in their cabs; you are a priest at the wheel, my friend, if you work with honesty, consecrating that taxi of yours to God, bearing a message of peace and love to the passengers who ride in your cab.   —November 20, 1977, *VL*, 11

It is very easy to be servants of the word without disturbing the world: a very spiritualized word, a word without any commitment to history, a word that can sound in any part of the world because it belongs to no part of the world. A word like that creates no problems, starts no conflicts.

What starts conflicts and persecutions, what marks the genuine church, is the word that, burning like the word of the prophets, proclaims and accuses: proclaims to the people God's wonders to be believed and venerated, and accuses of sin those who oppose God's reign, so that they may tear that sin out of their hearts, out of their societies, out of their laws — out of the structures that oppress, that imprison, that violate the rights of God and of humanity.

This is the hard service of the word.

But God's Spirit goes with the prophet, with the preacher, for he is Christ, who keeps on proclaiming his reign to the people of all times.

—December 10, 1977, *VL*, 18

The guarantee of one's prayer is not in saying a lot of words. The guarantee of one's petition is very easy to know: how do I treat the poor? Because that is where God is... What you do to them, you do to God. The way you look at them is the way you look at God.

—February 5, 1978, *VL*, 35

To pray is to converse with God. Vatican Council II uses a very helpful comparison saying that God has given humans the intimate sanctuary of their consciousness so that they can enter that private space and there speak alone with God to decide their own destiny. We all have a church within ourselves, our own consciousness. There God is, God's Spirit. Blessed are those who do not forsake that shrine by failing to pray. Blessed are those who enter often to speak along with their God. Try it yourselves, brothers and sisters.

Though you feel yourselves sinners, tainted, enter all the more and say: Lord, correct me, I have sinned, I have offended you.

Or when you feel the joy of a good act: Lord, I give you thanks because my conscience is joyful and you commend me.

Or when in affliction you find no one to offer a word of guidance, enter your intimate sanctuary, and God will show you the way.

Or when you are sad, like those many mothers of persons arrested and not seen again, enter alone with God and say: Lord, you know where they are. You know how they are being treated.

Speak with him. How beautiful is prayer, my friend, when it is truly made with God's Spirit inside us, and sharing in God's life!

—July 23, 1978, VL, 69

To each one of us Christ is saying: If you want your life and mission to be fruitful like mine, do as I. Be converted into seed that lets itself be buried. Let yourselves be killed. Do not be afraid. Those who shun suffering will remain alone. No one is more alone than the selfish. But if you give your life out of love for others, as I give mine for all, you will reap a great harvest. You will have the deepest satisfactions. Do not fear death or threats; the Lord goes with you.   —April 1, 1979, VL, 128

Christ invites us not to fear persecution. Believe me, brothers and sisters, anyone committed to the poor must suffer the same fate as the poor. And in El Salvador, we know the fate of the poor: to be taken away, to be tortured, to be jailed, to be found dead.   —February 17, 1980, VL, 192

THE POLITICAL DIMENSION OF FAITH

On February 2, 1980, Archbishop Romero delivered a talk at the Catholic University of Louvain in Belgium, where he was presented with an honorary degree. Thanking the university, he accepted the honor "as an eloquent testimony of support and fellowship toward my people's sufferings and their noble liberation struggle and as a gesture of communion and sympathy with the pastoral action of my archdiocese." He chose this occasion for a talk on "the political dimension of faith."

The Christian faith and the activity of the church have always had socio-political repercussions. By commission or omission, by associating themselves with one or another social group, Christians have always had an influence upon the socio-political makeup of the world in which they lived. The problem is about the "how" of this influence in the socio-political world, whether or not it is in accordance with the faith.

As a first idea, though still a very general one, I want to propose the intuition of Vatican II that lies at the root of every ecclesial movement of today. The essence of the church lies in its mission of service to the world, in its mission to save the world in its totality, and of saving it in history, here and now. The church exists to act in solidarity with the hopes and joys, the anxieties and sorrows, of men and women. Like Jesus, the church was sent "to bring good news to the poor, to heal the contrite of heart...to seek and to save what was lost" (Luke 4:18, 19:10).

You all know these words of Scripture, given prominence by Vatican II... My contribution will be to flesh out those beautiful declarations from the standpoint of my own situation, that of a small Latin American country, typical of what today is called the Third World. To put it in one word...the world that the church ought to serve is, for us, the world of the poor... And we say of that world of the poor that it is the key to understanding the Christian faith, to understanding the activity of the church and the political dimension of that faith and that ecclesial activity. It is the poor who tell us what the world is, and what the church's service to the world should be. It is the poor who tell us what the *polis* is, what the city is, and what it means for the church really to live in that world...

Our encounter with the poor has regained for us the central truth of the gospel, through which the word of God urges us to conversion. Those who, in this-worldly terms, have heard bad news, and who have lived out even worse realities, are now listening through the church to the word of Jesus: "The kingdom of God is at hand; blessed are you who are poor, for the kingdom of God is yours."...

Amos and Isaiah are not just voices from distant centuries; their writings are not merely texts that we reverently read in the liturgy. They are everyday realities. Day by day we live out the cruelty and ferocity they excoriate. We live them out when there come to us the mothers and the wives of those who have been arrested or who have disappeared, when mutilated bodies turn up in secret cemeteries, when those who fight for justice and peace are assassinated...

In this situation of conflict and antagonism, in which just a few persons control economic and political power, the church has placed itself at the side of the poor and has undertaken their defense. The church cannot do otherwise, for it remembers that Jesus had pity on the multitude. But by defending the poor it has entered into serious conflict with the powerful...

This defense of the poor in a world deep in conflict has occasioned something new in the recent history of our church: persecution. You know the more important facts. In less than three years over fifty priests have been attacked, threatened, calumniated. Six are already martyrs — they were murdered. Some have been tortured and others expelled. Nuns have also been persecuted...

If all this has happened to persons who are the most evident representatives of the church, you can guess what has happened to ordinary Christians... Persecution has been occasioned by the defense of the poor. It amounts to nothing other than the church's taking upon itself the lot of the poor.

Real persecution has been directed against the poor, the body of Christ in history today. They, like Jesus, are the crucified, the persecuted servant of Yahweh. They are the ones who make up in their own bodies that which is lacking in the passion of Christ. And for that reason when the church has organized and united itself around the hopes and the anxieties of the poor, it has incurred the same fate as that of Jesus and of the poor: persecution.

The course taken by the archdiocese has clearly issued from its faith conviction... But it is also true... that the faith itself has been deepened, that hidden riches of the gospel have been opened, precisely by taking up this stance toward socio-political reality such as it is...

In the first place, we have a better knowledge of what sin is. We know that offending God is death for humans. We know that such a sin really is mortal, not only in the sense of the interior death of the person who commits the sin, but also because of the real, objective death the sin produces. Let us remind ourselves of a fundamental datum of our Christian faith: sin killed the Son of God, and sin is what goes on killing the children of God.

We see that basic truth of the Christian faith daily in the situation in our country. It is impossible to offend God without offending one's brother or sister. And the worst offense against God, the worst form of secularism, as one of our Salvadoran theologians has said, is "to turn children of God, temples of the Holy Spirit, the body of Christ in history, into victims of oppression and injustice, into slaves to economic greed, into fodder for political repression..."

It is not a matter of sheer routine that I insist once again on the existence in our country of structures of sin. They are sin because they produce the fruits of sin: the deaths of Salvadorans — the swift death brought by repression or the long, drawn out, but no less real, death from structural oppression...

In the second place we now have a better understanding of what the incarnation means, what it means to say that Jesus really took human flesh and made himself one with his brothers and sisters in suffering, in tears and laments, in surrender. I am not speaking of universal incarnation. This is impossible. I am speaking of an incarnation that is preferential and partial: incarnation in the world of the poor...

The world of the poor, with its very concrete social and political characteristics, teaches us where the church can incarnate itself in such a way that it will avoid the false universalism that inclines the church to associate itself with the powerful. The world of the poor teaches us what the nature of Christian love is, a love that certainly seeks peace but also unmasks false pacifism — the pacifism of resignation and inactivity. It is a love that should certainly be freely offered, but that seeks to be effective in history. The world of the poor teaches us that the sublimity of Christian love ought to be mediated through the overriding necessity of justice for the majority. It ought not to turn away from honorable conflict. The world of the poor teaches us that liberation will arrive only when the poor are not simply on the receiving end of handouts from governments or from the church, but when they themselves are the masters of, and protagonists in, their own struggle and liberation, thereby unmasking the root of false paternalism, including ecclesiastical paternalism.

The real world of the poor also teaches us about Christian hope. The church preaches a new heaven and a new earth. It knows, moreover, that no socio-political system can be exchanged for the final fullness that is given by God. But it has also learned that transcendent hope must be preserved by signs of hope in history, no matter how simply they may apparently be — such as those proclaimed by the Trito-Isaiah when he says "they will build houses and inhabit them, plant vineyards and eat their fruit" (Isa. 65:21). What in this is an authentically Christian hope... is being learned daily through contact with those who have no houses and no vineyards, those who build for others to inhabit and work so that others may eat the fruits.

In the third place, incarnation in the socio-political world is the locus for deepening faith in God and in his Christ. We believe in Jesus who came to bring the fullness of life, and we believe in a living God who gives life to men and women and wants them truly to live. These radical truths of the faith become really true and truly radical when the church enters into the heart of the life and death of its people. Then there is put before the faith of the church, as it is put before the faith of every individual, the most fundamental choice: to be in favor of life or to be in favor of death. We see, with great clarity, that here neutrality is impossible. Either we serve the life of Salvadorans, or we are accomplices in their death. And here what is most fundamental about the faith is given expression in history: either we believe in a God of life, or we serve the idols of death.

In the name of Jesus we want, and we work for, life in its fullness, a life that is not reduced to the frantic search for basic material needs, nor one reduced to the sphere of the socio-political. We know perfectly well that the superabundant fullness of life is to be achieved only in the kingdom of the Father. In human history this fullness is achieved through a worthy service of that kingdom, and total surrender to the Father. But we see with equal clarity that in the name of Jesus it would be sheer illusion, it would be an irony, and, at bottom, it would be the most profound blasphemy, to forget and to ignore the basic levels of life, the life that begins with bread, a roof, a job...

This faith in the God of life is the explanation for what lies deepest in the Christian mystery. To give life to the poor one has to give of one's own life, even to give one's life itself. The greatest sign of faith in a God of life is the witness of those who are ready to give up their own life. "A man can have no greater love than to lay down his life for his friends" (John 15:13). And we see this daily in our country. Many Salvadorans, many Christians, are ready to give their lives so that the poor may have life. They are following Jesus and showing their faith in him. Living within the real world just as Jesus did, like him accused and threatened, like him laying down their lives, they are giving witness to the Word of life...

Early Christians used to say *Gloria Dei, vivens homo* ("the glory of God is the living person"). We could make this more concrete by saying *Gloria Dei, vivens pauper* ("the glory of God is the living poor person"). From the perspective of the transcendence of the gospel, I believe we can determine what the life of the poor truly is. And I also believe that by putting ourselves alongside the poor and trying to bring life to them we shall come to know the eternal truth of the gospel.

— "The Political Dimension of the Faith from the Perspective of the Option for the Poor," Louvain Address, February 2, 1980, *VV*

FROM HIS FINAL SERMON

On Sunday, March 23, 1980, Romero preached his final Sunday sermon. This sermon, broadcast on radio, ended with an impassioned plea to the country's armed forces to refuse to persecute their own people. In retrospect, his words may have signed his own death warrant. He was assassinated the next day while saying Mass.

I have been trying during these Sundays of Lent to uncover in divine revelation, the word read here at Mass, God's program to save peoples and individuals. Today, when history offers our people various proposals, we can say with assurance: the program that better reflects God's program will prevail. And this is the church's mission. And so, in the light of God's word revealing God's plan for the happiness of peoples, we have the duty of also pointing out the realities, of seeing how God's plan is reflected among us or despised among us. Let no one take it ill that in the light of God's words read in our Mass we illuminate social, political, and economic realities. If we did not, this would not be our own Christianity. It is thus that Christ willed to become incarnate, so that the light that he brings from the Father may become the life of people and of nations.

I know that many are scandalized at what I say and charge that it forsakes the preaching of the gospel to meddle in politics. I do not accept that accusation. No, I strive that we may not just have on paper and study in theory all that Vatican Council II and the meetings at Medellín and Puebla have tried to further in us, but that we may live it and interpret it in this conflict-ridden reality, preaching the gospel as it should be preached for our people. I ask the Lord during the week, while I gather the people's cries and the sorrow stemming from so much crime, the ignominy of so much violence, to give me the fitting word to console, to denounce, to call to repentance. And though I continue to be a voice that cries in the desert, I know that the church is making the effort to fulfill its mission...

I would like to appeal in a special way to the army's enlisted men, and in particular to the ranks of the Guardia Nacional and the police — those in the barracks. Brothers: you are part of our own people. You kill your own campesino brothers and sisters. And before an order to kill that a man may give, God's law must prevail that says: Thou shalt not kill! No soldier is obliged to obey an order against the law of God. No one has to fulfill an immoral law. It is time to take back your consciences and to obey your consciences rather than the orders of sin. The church, defender of the rights of God, of the law of God, of human dignity, of the person, cannot remain silent before such abomination. We want the government to understand seriously that reforms are worth nothing if they are stained with so much blood. In the name of God, and in the name of this suffering people, whose laments rise to heaven each day more tumultuous, I beg you, I beseech you, I order you in the name of God: Stop the repression.   — *Romero, 240–42*

MARTYRDOM

How sad it would be, in a country where such horrible murders are being committed, if there were no priests among the victims! They are the testimony of a church incarnated in the problems of its people.

— *OR, 86*

To his spiritual director a few weeks before his death

It is not easy to accept a violent death, which is very possible in these circumstances... You have encouraged me, reminding me that my attitude should be to hand my life over to God regardless of the end to which that life might come; that unknown circumstances can be faced with God's grace; that God assisted the martyrs, and that if it comes to this I shall feel God very close as I draw my last breath; but that more valiant than surrender in death is the surrender of one's whole life — a life lived for God.   — *OR, 99–100*

From an interview two weeks before his death

I have often been threatened with death. I must tell you, as a Christian, I do not believe in death without resurrection. If I am killed, I shall arise in the Salvadoran people. I say so without boasting, with the greatest humility.

As a shepherd, I am obliged by divine mandate to give my life for those I love — for all Salvadorans, even for those who may be going to kill me. If the threats are carried out, from this moment I offer my blood to God for the redemption and for the resurrection of El Salvador.

Martyrdom is a grace of God that I do not believe I deserve. But if God accepts the sacrifice of my life, let my blood be a seed of freedom and the sign that hope will soon be reality. Let my death, if it is accepted by God, be for my people's liberation and as a witness of hope in the future.

You may say, if they succeed in killing me, that I pardon and bless those who do it. Would, indeed, that they might be convinced that they will waste their time. A bishop will die, but God's church, which is the people, will never perish. — *Romero*, 247–48

The word remains. This is the great comfort of one who preaches. My voice will disappear, but my word, which is Christ, will remain in the hearts of those who have willed to receive it.

—December 17, 1978, *Romero*, ii

SOURCES

OR   Marie Dennis, Renny Golden, Scott Wright, *Oscar Romero: Reflections on His Life and Writings* (Maryknoll, NY: Orbis Books, 2000).

Romero   James R. Brockman, *Romero: A Life* (Maryknoll, NY: Orbis Books, 1989).

VL   Oscar Romero, *The Violence of Love,* compiled and translated by James R. Brockman (Maryknoll, NY: Orbis Books, 2004).

VV   Oscar Romero, *Voice of the Voiceless: The Four Pastoral Letters and Other Statements* (Maryknoll, NY: Orbis Books, 1985).

SIX

CATHERINE
DE HUECK DOHERTY
The Gospel without Compromise

◙⌸⌸⌸⌸⌸⌸⌸⌸◙

Catherine Kolyschkine, as she was first named, was born in Russia on the feast of the Assumption in 1896. Her father, a wealthy diplomat and industrialist, was half-Polish and Catholic, and so Catherine was raised in the Catholic church. When she was fifteen she married Baron Boris de Hueck, which made her a baroness. No sooner had she made this entry into the aristocracy than Russia was plunged into the First World War. While the baron served as an officer on the front, Catherine worked as a nurse. They watched as the starving and demoralized Russian army began to retreat, presaging the collapse of the tsarist empire in the October Revolution of 1917.

Though Catherine and Boris were reunited, their situation, as aristocrats, was perilous. Deprived of food rations, they came close to starving before risking a hazardous flight across the border to Finland. By 1920 they had arrived with their newborn son in Canada. Still in desperate financial straits, Catherine traveled to New York in search of work. She held a number of low-paying jobs. Finally, while working as a department store sales clerk, she was approached by a woman who asked if it was true that she was a Russian baroness, and would she be interested in lecturing about her experiences. Catherine immediately agreed, and soon she was on a lecture circuit, making $300 a week describing her harrowing escape from communism. During this time her marriage collapsed. It seemed that she had finally put the memory of poverty and hunger behind her. She had a luxurious apartment, a fancy car, and a country house — all that communism had taken away from her. And yet her conscience was clouded by a nagging doubt, a feeling that it was just such a materialistic life and the failure of Christian values that had fed the communist revolution.

At the peak of her success she felt the pull of the gospel verse, "Go, sell what you have and give to the poor. Then come follow me." So in 1930 she gave up her worldly goods and moved into an apartment in the slums of Toronto, committed to living "the gospel without compromise." With the support of the archbishop, she came to establish Friendship House, a storefront center for the works of mercy, where the hungry were fed and the homeless were welcomed. Catherine's program of action was simple and unsystematic. It was merely a matter of living among the poor with an open door and an open heart. There was no need to seek out people in need. They came to her.

She received encouragement in these years from Dorothy Day, whose Catholic Worker movement was operating on similar principles in New York's Bowery. In 1937 Catherine herself moved to New York to establish a Friendship House in Harlem. She had come to feel that the sin of racial prejudice and the consequent segregation of whites and blacks was the greatest countersign to the gospel. Friendship House was a sign of interracial justice and reconciliation.

Among those moved by her example was the young Thomas Merton, who heard Catherine speak in 1938 and who joined her for a time in Harlem. Years later, in his autobiography, he described her message:

> Catholics are worried about Communism: and they have a right to be . . . But few Catholics stop to think that Communism would make very little progress in the world, or none at all, if Catholics really lived up to their obligations, and really did the things Christ came on earth to teach them to do: that is, if they really loved one another, and saw Christ in one another, and lived as saints, and did something to win justice for the poor.

Catherine was a large woman whose bearing of authority, commanding presence, and thick Russian accent all seemed appropriate to the title of Baroness. That is indeed how most people addressed her. But to her friends she was simply "the B." She was famous for her earthy humor and her righteous anger. When a society woman sniffed contemptuously, "You smell of the Negro," Catherine retorted, "And you stink of hell!"

Nevertheless, her imperious style of leadership led to tensions. In 1946 Catherine resigned from Friendship House. By this time she had married a famous journalist, Eddie Doherty. Together they moved back to

Ontario, Canada, and settled on a piece of land in the forests of Comber-mere. Catherine established a new community called Madonna House, which became a place of prayer and retreat. At Madonna House she returned full circle to the atmosphere of Russian spirituality she had known in her youth. Out of this came her best-selling book, Poustinia. *The "poustinia," the Russian word for desert, is a place of silence and withdrawal from the compulsions of the world, a place to listen to God. It could be a hut in the forest, a special room in our apartment, or even a special place within our hearts, to which from time to time we might re-treat. Through Madonna House and the communities it inspired around the world, Catherine promoted the two principles by which she lived — a commitment to the social apostolate in the world and the need to root such a commitment in a life of prayer and the spirit of Christ.*

She died on December 14, 1985.

DESERT SILENCE

For the last few years I have been talking and writing a great deal about silence, solitude, and deserts, and I will continue to write about them because I think they are vitally important to our growing, changing, technological, urban civilization. It is obvious that humanity is facing many problems, will have to face many more, and that these problems are deeply disturbing the souls of all men. It is just as certain that we cannot, must not, reject the new, strange, adventuresome, frightening world that is opening before us...that is already with us. Especially we Christians cannot do this because Christ has inserted himself into this world and we are his people, his body, and so we belong as he does to this world...

It seems strange to say, but what can help modern man find the an-swers to his own mystery and the mystery of him in whose image he is created, is *silence, solitude — in a word, the desert.* Modern man needs these things more than the hermits of old.

If we are to witness to Christ in today's marketplaces, where there are constant demands of our whole person, we need silence. If we are to be always available, not only physically, but by empathy, sympathy, friendship, understanding and boundless *caritas,* we need silence. To be able to give joyous, unflagging hospitality, not only of house and food, but of mind, heart, body and soul, we need silence.

True silence is the search of man for God.

True silence is a suspension bridge that a soul in love with God builds to cross the dark, frightening gullies of its own mind, the strange chasms of temptation, the depthless precipices of its own fears that impede its way to God.

True silence is the speech of lovers. For only love knows its beauty, completeness, and utter joy. True silence is a garden enclosed, where alone the soul can meet its God. It is a sealed foundation that he alone can unseal to slacken the soul's infinite thirst for him.

True silence is a key to the immense and flaming heart of God. It is the beginning of a divine courtship that will end only in the immense, creative, fruitful, loving silence of final union with the Beloved.

Yes, such silence is holy, a prayer beyond all prayers, leading to the final prayer of constant presence of God, to the heights of contemplation, when the soul, finally at peace, lives by the will of him whom she loves totally, utterly, and completely.

This silence, then, will break forth in a charity that overflows in the service of the neighbor without counting the cost. It will witness to Christ anywhere, always. Availability will become delightsome and easy, for in each person the soul will see the face of her Love. Hospitality will be deep and real, for a silent heart is a loving heart, and a loving heart is a hospice to the world.

This silence is not the exclusive prerogative of monasteries or convents. This simple, prayerful silence is everybody's silence — or if it isn't, it should be. It belongs to every Christian who loves God, to every Jew who has heard in his heart the echoes of God's voice in his prophets, to everyone whose soul has risen in search of truth, in search of God. For where noise is — inward noise and confusion — there God is not!

Deserts, silence, solitudes are *not necessarily places but states of mind and heart.* These deserts can be found in the midst of the city, and in the everyday of our lives. We need only to look for them and realize our tremendous need for them. They will be small solitudes, little deserts, tiny pools of silence, but the experience they will bring, if we are disposed to enter them, may be as exultant and as holy as all the deserts of the world, even the one God himself entered. For it is God who makes solitude, deserts, and silences holy.

Consider the solitude of walking from the subway train or bus to your home in the evening, when the streets are quiet and there are few passersby. Consider the solitude that greets you when you enter your room to change your office or working clothes to more comfortable, homey ones ... Think of the solitudes afforded by such humble tasks as housecleaning, ironing, sewing.

One of the first steps toward solitude is a departure. Were you to depart to a real desert, you might take a plane, train, or car to get there. But we're blind to the "little departures" that fill our days. These "little solitudes" are often right behind a door which we can open, or in a little corner where we can stop to look at a tree that somehow survived the snow and dust of a city street. There is the solitude of a car in which we return from work, riding bumper to bumper on a crowded highway. This too can be a "point of departure" to a desert, silence, solitude.

But our hearts, minds, and souls must be attuned, desirous, aware of these moments of solitude that God gives us. To be so attuned we must lose our superstition of time. God laughs at time, for if our souls are open to him, available to him, he can invite them, change them, lift them, transform them in *one instant*! He can say to someone driving that car bumper to bumper, "I will lead you into solitude and there I shall speak to your heart" (Hos. 2:14).

There is no solitude without silence. True, silence is sometimes the absence of speech — but it is always the act of listening. The mere absence of noise (which is empty of our listening to the voice of God) is not silence. A day filled with noise and voices can be a day of silence, if the noises become for us the echo of the presence of God, if the voices are, for us, messages and solicitations of God. When we speak of ourselves and are filled with ourselves, we leave silence behind. When we repeat the intimate words of God that he has left within us, our silence remains intact.

Silence is truth in charity. It answers him who asks. But it must give only words filled with light. Silence, like everything else, either makes us give ourselves, or it becomes miserliness and avarice, in which we keep ourselves to ourselves. The scripture says that we will have to give an account for every word. Perhaps we may also have to render an account for the words that we have not spoken and should have!

Deserts, silence, solitude. For a soul that realizes the tremendous need of all three, opportunities present themselves in the midst of the congested trappings of all the world's immense cities.

But how, really, can one achieve such solitude? *By standing still!* Stand still, and allow the strange, deadly restlessness of our tragic age to fall away like the worn-out dusty cloak that it is — a cloak that was once considered beautiful. The restlessness was considered the magic carpet to tomorrow, but now in reality we see it for what it is: a running away from oneself, a turning from that journey inward that all men must undertake to meet God dwelling within the depths of their souls.

Stand still, and look deep into the motivations of life. Are they such that true foundations of sanctity can be built on them? For truly man has been born to be a saint — a lover of Love who died for us! There is but one tragedy: not to be a saint. If these motivations of life are not such that they can be true foundations for sanctity, then the soul must start all over again and find other motivations. It can be done. It must be done. It is never too late to begin again.

Stand still, and lifting your hearts and hands to God, pray that the mighty wind of his Holy Spirit may clear all the cobwebs of fear, selfishness, greed, narrow-heartedness away from the soul: that his tongues of flame may descend to give courage to begin again.

All this standing still can be done in the midst of the outward noise of daily living and the duties of one's state in life. For it will bring order into the soul, God's order, and God's order will bring tranquility, his own tranquility. And it will bring silence.

It will bring the silence of a lover listening with all his being to the heartbeats of his beloved. The silence of a bride who, in her utter joy, listens to her heart reechoing every word of the beloved. The silence of a mother, so deep, so inward, that in it she listens with her whole being to the voice of her children playing in a nearby yard, cognizant without effort, for the slightest change in each voice. Hers is a listening silence which takes place while she competently, efficiently, and lovingly attends to her daily duties...

At first such silences will be few and far between. But if nourished with a life of liturgical prayer, mental prayer, with the sacramental life of the Church, slowly, slowly, like the seedling of a mighty tree, silence will grow and come to dwell in a soul more and more often. Then suddenly, it will come to stay one day...

Nourished by the waters of silence, *caritas* will begin to sing its song of love, making all men and women literally spend themselves for others — at home, abroad, in any and every state of life, on all streets and marketplaces of the world. And Lo! Behold. Their strength — even as their youth — will be renewed as an eagle's!

Slowly, imperceptibly, the world roundabout them will change. For the silence within them will become part of God's loving, mighty, creative, fruitful silence. His voice will be heard through them. His face will be seen in theirs! And the light of it will become a light to their neighbor's feet.

Thus silence will bring peace to all. The prayer of silence will be heard in our land far and wide. And the Beloved will once more come to dwell among men, for his vineyard — the world — will be restored to him. Yes, "Be still, and know that I am God" (Ps. 46:10).   — *Poustinia*, 18–25

What is the answer to all these darknesses that press so heavily on us?...

I think I have one answer — *the poustinia*...Poustinia stands for prayer, penance, mortification, solitude, silence, offered in the spirit of love, atonement, and reparation to God...

The word "poustinia" is Russian meaning "desert." It is an ordinary word...The word to the Russian means much more than a geographical place. It means a quiet, lonely place that people wish to enter, to find the God who dwells within them. It also means truly isolated, lonely places to which specially called people would go as hermits and would seek God in solitude, silence and prayer for the rest of their lives!

However, a poustinia was not necessarily completely away from the haunts of men. Some people had reserved in their homes, a small room to which they went to pray and meditate, which some might call a poustinia.   — *Poustinia*, 29–31

I have always been attracted to the silence and solitude of God. Even when it became obvious that my vocation was not to be physical silence and solitude, and when I was thrown into the noisiest marketplaces in the world, God showed me how to live out the poustinia ideal...

There will always be "solitaries," or should be. But the essence of the poustinia is that it is a place within oneself, a result of Baptism, where each of us contemplates the Trinity. Within my heart, within me, I am or should be constantly in the presence of God. This is another way of saying that I live in a garden enclosed, where I walk and talk with God (though a Russian would say "where all in me is silent and where I am immersed in the silence of God"). It's as if I were sitting next to God in complete silence, although there are always many other people around...

Like the poustinik, I go about God's business all day long. The poustinik enters his poustinia and takes humanity with him. He lifts that humanity before God, with all its pain, sorrows, joys, everything. John Howard Griffin wrote a book called *Black Like Me*. He told how he changed his skin pigmentation into a dark color so that he could really identify with the Black people. A poustinik thus identifies himself with humanity. He *becomes* the Black man, the minority group, the poor, the restless rich — he *is* everyone! By his inner solitude, the poustinik identifies himself with God. Thus identified, he becomes one with the God who became Man.

The poustinia is within and one is forever immersed in the silence of God, forever listening to the word of God, forever repeating it to others in word and deed... The poustinia is this inner solitude, this inner immersion in the silence of God. It is through this inner, total identification with humanity and with Christ that every Christian should be living in a state of contemplation. This is the poustinia within oneself.

The poustinia is a state of constantly being in the presence of God because one desires him with a great desire, because in him alone can one rest. The poustinia is walking in this inner solitude, immersed in the silence of God. My life of silence and love to my fellowman is simply the echo of this silence and solitude. Inwardly I identify myself with God and with humanity. Jesus Christ himself conducts me into this inner silence, into that solitude which speaks so loudly to the Father under the guidance of the Holy Spirit. Now I am immersed in the Trinity, in the fire of the silence of God (for the silence of God is always fire; his speech is fire). Now I become as one on fire with love of him and of all humanity across the world...   — *Poustinia*, 211–14

PRAYER

God has given this day into our hands. This is the day in which we pray, but we pray by action and sweat, just as Christ did. He said he "came not to be served but to serve" (Matt. 20:28). He also said, "Pray continually" (Luke 18:1). Pray while you work and work while you pray.

The duty of the moment is our strategic place. One day at a time. We have this day in which to open our hearts like doors, and take in everyone that we can. Today we have to love as God loved us.

Some feel as if the routine of our daily duties is not enough, that other things should be added. Stop here. Please stop. Fall on your knees and pray and listen. Walk slowly, in the darkness of faith — because you believe in the Trinity, for no other reason. Then, through hope and love, be faithful to your duty of the present moment. That is the essence of Christianity. That is the heart of the Church. The rest flows from it, but this is to come first, walking in faith while doing our daily routine of duties.

It might seem strange but it is the fruit of that faith and hope that the Lord, bending, picks up. With this fruit, he changes the world and allows his Church to expand, because one, two, three, or more people believe, hope, and love.

Our daily work, routine or not, exciting or unexciting, monotonous or not, is part of that faith, hope, and love. This workaday world of ours is the outer shell of a deep inner grace that God gives us. It is because we believe, we hope, and we love that we can do what might seem impossible.

Christ wants us to be an icon of himself, to be people of faith beyond reason, to be fools for God in utter simplicity, and to be people who plead for others in prayer.   — *Living*, 141–42

GOSPEL WITHOUT COMPROMISE

There is no denying that I am a modern traveler... Everywhere I went ... there was one main topic of conversation in our day and age. That topic is *God*.

Yes, my deepest impression from my travels was that man's hunger for God is at its peak, but that Christians do not know how to fill this hunger. Maybe it's because they do not *recognize* this hunger for what it is, and thus do not realize how to fill it.

But let's face it. If the world is atheistic, if much of it has not yet heard the Good News, or if it has heard but not accepted it, then the main fault lies with us Christians who have not lived the gospel. We have only filled the libraries of the world with books which have more or less watered down the message of the gospel.

Christianity has become an affair of ethical, moral behavior. An affair of going to Church, of learning rules to make sure that one will get to heaven. The gap between the reality of the gospel and the teaching contained in all those library volumes has reaped its harvest of damage...

We should stop talking about God and start living out the gospel in our lives, manifesting the image of the Lord so clearly in our hearts that no one can possibly say that he is dead. We should stop worrying about theological theory and begin building among ourselves communities of love.

We live in Pentecostal times. Once again the invincible love of the Holy Spirit is among us. We have only to open our hearts to it and we shall change the world. Then our own hearts will contain the fire and flame that Jesus sent to renew the earth.

When the apostles went to preach the Good News and to baptize as the Lord instructed them, they didn't have any catechetical manuals. They had the gospel. They had the Holy Spirit. They brought the kingdom of Christ to an immense portion of the then-known world.

Why can't we modern Christians adopt the "techniques" of the apostles and of the early Christians? True, we may wind up in some prisons, prisons of rejection, ridicule, and maybe even physical prisons.

We may be crucified in a thousand ways, maybe even locked up in psychiatric wards as St. Francis might be if he were alive today. But so what? The gospel would be preached to the poor and the kingdom of God would begin at least to have a toehold in our modern world. Yes, Jesus came to cast fire on the earth. Would that this fire was enkindled in our hearts today! — *GWC*, 15–17

God asked Cain where his brother Abel was. And Cain answered, "Am I my brother's keeper?" To how many of us today could God address the same question, and how many of us might give the same answer? Cain slew his brother because he envied him. We kill our brothers, slowly, deliberately, almost with malice aforethought. This is not because we, the affluent nations, envy other people. No. We have left them in a state where no one can really envy them. No. We are killing, meting out death, not because of envy, but because of avarice and greed.

We have given mere pennies for the raw materials of poor nations and charged dollars for the processed goods. We knew full well that without "purchase pennies" their standard of living would not improve, and slowly, through much misery and pain, they would come to death by starvation. Then we would put on the mask of charity, benignly bestowing a few million, or even billions that we could easily afford but which would not solve their pain, nor alleviate their misery.

Am I my brother's keeper? If we truly examined our Western conscience — the conscience of the so-called affluent society — we would be trembling indeed. It would be clear that we have slain our brother by enlarging our profits. Our profits! That is all we care about these days . . .

Am I my brother's keeper? Oh no! I am my brother's killer! . . .

But at long last my brothers of the poor nations are slowly gathering, gathering to face us. The confrontation will be terrible. For as we look at this incredibly immense gathering of our poor brothers (whom we have exploited to the limit of anybody's endurance), they will suddenly turn into the figure of Christ — all of them — a Christ armed with cords. He will chase us, the traffickers in his temple, the moneylenders, the death-sellers, with the cords of his wrath which we so justly deserve.

— *GWC*, 29–30

I have often spoken of identification with the poor. By that I mean an identification of love that is color-blind. It is an identification that only love can achieve by complete forgetfulness of self and total concern for the other person. It is an identification so deep, so complete, that it becomes part of oneself — like breathing! It is a way of love that is willing — nay, eager — to be a Simon of Cyrene to the passion of Christ in men. Not reluctantly, but eagerly and joyfully, this love picks up the cross carried by the neighbor — the heavy cross of pain, sorrow, and fear, and shares the weight of it as far as is humanly possible — and a little beyond!

This identification is a love that incarnates the abstract words we use so glibly every day — "sympathy," "empathy," "understanding." It makes them come alive under its touch. It is a personalized love that never counts the loss of giving.

This type of identification also entails a change of life-style. One must live like those with whom one wishes to identify. It would have been impossible to identify ourselves with the Negroes in Harlem *if we had not lived in Harlem.* We had to be poor as they were poor. We had to experience the way of life they experienced. We had to experience the crowded apartments with their poor ventilation; unbearably hot in the summer and unbearably cold in the winter. We had to experience the poor plumbing, which, at times, could threaten our very lives...

Because we identified in these ways, those who received things from us did not hate us. They began to love us. The law of love, the law of Christ, began to work in Harlem in a tangible way. This was the cement of the whole structure of love, of the whole apostolate. Such cement is not easy to make. Its source is God, and prayer was the channel through which it came to us from him.   — *Fragments,* 159–60

LOVE

Christians are called to become icons of Christ, to reflect him. But we are called to even more than that. *Ikon* is the Greek word for "image of God." We are called to incarnate him in our lives, to clothe our lives with him, so that men can see him in us, touch him in us, recognize him in us.

When we don't live the gospel without compromise, or try to, we are skeletons. People do not care to deal with skeletons. The gospel can be summed up by saying that it is the tremendous, tender, compassionate, gentle, extraordinary, explosive, revolutionary law of Christ's love.

He calls each one of us who calls himself a Christian. He calls us directly. There is no compromise in his call: "Whoever is not with me is against me...If you love me, keep my commandments." We can find umpteen quotations in the gospel that will vividly bring forth to our minds and hearts how simply and how insistently he calls us to be like him, and to accept his law of love without compromise.

His call is revolutionary, there is no denying it. If we Christians implemented it, it would change the world in a few months. The gospel is radical, and Christ indeed is the *radix*, the root from which spring all things. His commandments mean risk, great risk. They imply a lack of that security to which most men cling so tightly...

God offers us risk, danger and a strange insecurity that leads to perfect security. His security begins when we start loving God with our whole heart, our whole mind, our whole soul and our neighbor as ourselves. I speak of this so often but it is the only message that can never be overstressed. We must clothe the skeletons of our lives with the flesh of his love, or we shall perish...

All this sounds very idealistic and perhaps quite unobtainable. Christ assures us it *is* attainable. It is through those strange little steps day after day that one slowly accepts the other as he or she is, begins to love totally, tenderly, compassionately. Once this has begun, the involvement becomes deeper and deeper and deeper.

As this involvement of love between brothers grows and deepens, we enter into a revolution. A revolution in which there is a violence directed only against oneself. There is much to be overcome, so terribly much, before we can say with St. Paul, "I live now, not I, but Christ lives in me." This kind of warfare truly brings about a revolution in the individual and in the community of mankind. The revolution of Christ brings about a whole new set of values.

My brothers and sisters in Christ, I implore you before it is too late, clothe the skeletons of your flesh with the love of Christ. If we do, we can lead the world and humanity out of the terrible and hellish depths to which it has sunk. There is so little time.   — *GWC,* 71–73

It seems that it is time for all of us Christians to face God and to tell him, "Yes, Lord, we are with you, for where else can we go?" or to say, "No, Lord, your sayings are too hard, and we shall not follow you any longer."

A sense of deep sadness comes over me when I think of how Christians sit on the fence. What is the matter with us? Have we forgotten that we are followers of a crucified Christ? Have we forgotten that he was just the son of a carpenter, himself a tradesman, a strange itinerant preacher who crisscrossed the tiny country of Palestine, preaching his gospel to the poor? Have we forgotten that from the moment he began preaching he walked in the shadow of death? Have we forgotten that following him means to take the greatest risk that man can take? Have we forgotten that following him means living dangerously?

It seems that we have spent centuries trying to eliminate the risk and the danger of his call. It seems that we have cushioned the risk and practically eliminated any and all danger by drawing up a set of moral rules that give us security instead of holy insecurity; rules that lull our conscience to sleep instead of making it wide awake and ready to undertake the risks of being a Christian.

Christ said that if we are not with him we are against him. How do we measure up to this saying of his? Are we really *with* him? . . .

We have to begin to love one another in the fullest sense of Christ's teaching. But to do so we must pray. It is only through prayer that one can follow Christ to Golgotha and up onto the other side of his cross, and to become free through his ascension. The immense problems of war, of social injustice, of the thousand and one ills that beset our world, these can be solved only if we begin to love one another. When man begins to see love, respect, and reverence Christ in the eyes of another, then he will change, and society will change also.

Christians must openly declare their allegiance to Christ, or their nonallegiance to him. The story of the disciples who had to choose is repeating itself today among us. "Who do *you* say that I am?" Peter, for the other disciples, openly declared himself for Jesus. On another occasion, Christ's words were too harsh, and other disciples admitted it and left him. It is time we did likewise and stopped fooling around. If ever there was a time when humanity needed followers of Christ and fewer fence-sitters, that time is now...

"What are we to do about Christianity?" Perhaps that is the wrong question. Perhaps we should ask ourselves, are we Christians?...

To be a Christian means to live in such a faith, in such commitment to Christ, that it will revolutionize, turn upside down not only our lives but the lives of others.

To be a Christian means to incarnate, actualize, literally implement the teachings of the gospel. It means preaching the gospel with one's life. This alone would be a revolution... — *GWC*, 74–76, 90

SOURCES

Fragments   *Fragments of My Life* (Notre Dame, IN: Ave Maria Press, 1979).

GWC   *The Gospel without Compromise* (Combermere, Ontario: Madonna House Publications, 1989).

Living   *Living the Gospel without Compromise* (Combermere, Ontario: Madonna House Publications, 2002).

Poustinia   *Poustinia: Christian Spirituality of the East for Western Man* (Notre Dame, IN: Ave Maria Press, 1975).

SEVEN

HOWARD THURMAN

Good News for the Disinherited

Howard Thurman (1899–1981), mystic, theologian, minister, and activist, was born in segregated Daytona Beach, Florida. He was raised by his mother and his grandmother—the latter, a former slave. His grandmother set a particular example of courage and faith. From her, he wrote, "I learned more…about the genius of the religion of Jesus…than from all the men who taught me all the Greek and all the rest of it. Because she moved inside the experience and lived out of that kind of center." Although his grandmother could neither read nor write, it was also she who inspired his love of learning.

Thurman received a full scholarship to study at Morehouse College in Atlanta, and later he prepared for ministry at Rochester Theological Seminary in Rochester, New York (where, due to quotas of the time, he was one of only two black students in his class). He later taught religion at Morehouse and Howard University.

A turning point in his life came in 1935 when he and his wife went on a pilgrimage for six months to India, Burma, and Ceylon. India was then in the midst of its struggle for independence, and the high point of Thurman's travel was the opportunity to meet with Mohandas Gandhi. Gandhi was eager to learn about the condition of black Americans, and he suggested that the principles of nonviolence might prove relevant to their struggle for civil rights. Thurman in turn described the religion forged in slavery and sang several spirituals, including "Were You There When They Crucified My Lord?" (In one of his early books, reflecting on the spiritual heritage of slaves, he wrote: "And this is the miracle of their achievement causing them to take their place alongside the great

*creative religious thinkers of the human race. They made a worthless
life, the life of chattel property, a mere thing, a body, worth living!")*

On his return, Thurman spoke widely about Gandhi and his tech-
nique of nonviolent resistance. Thus, he became an early link between
Gandhi's philosophy of nonviolence and the later civil rights movement.
But Thurman's travels also caused him to think more critically about
Christianity and its compromises with social injustice. From this reflection came his most influential work, Jesus and the Disinherited, which
examined the ministry of Jesus as a resource for resolving the race crisis.
The central question was, "What . . . is the word of the religion of Jesus
to those who stand with their backs against the wall?"

Thurman saw Jesus as himself a member of an oppressed people, living under Roman occupation. From this standpoint he examined the
parallels between the situation of Jesus and the condition of the disinherited in the world today. He also distinguished between the religion of
Jesus and the institution of Christianity.

Thurman served from 1953 to 1963 as dean of Marsh Chapel at Boston University. His first year coincided with Martin Luther King Jr.'s
last year as a doctoral student, and King credited Thurman as one of his
inspirations. He was later said to carry Jesus and the Disinherited with
him on demonstrations in the South.

In 1944 Thurman had helped form an interracial and intercultural
church, the Church for the Fellowship of All Peoples, in San Francisco.
He returned there after his retirement from Boston University and there
remained until his death in 1981.

Thurman wrote twenty books, many dealing with the nature of religious experience. In its profoundest dimension this religious experience
was "the finding of man by God and the finding of God by man."
Though Thurman always held in balance a concern for spirituality and
the social dimension, he wrote with the sensibility of a mystic. This was
not a matter of visions and ecstasies, but an intense awareness of a "conscious and direct exposure" to God. In this relationship, he wrote, we
find our true dignity and the sacred core of our being: "There must be
always remaining in every man's life some place for the singing of angels,
some place for that which in itself is breathlessly beautiful and, by an
inherent prerogative, throws all the rest of life into a new and creative
relatedness . . . A crown is placed over our heads that for the rest of our
lives we are trying to grow tall enough to wear. Despite all the crassness*

of life, despite all the hardness of life, despite all the harsh discords of life, life is saved by the singing of angels."

ENCOUNTERING GOD

The source of life is God. The mystic applies this to human life when he says that there is in man an uncreated element, or in the Book of Job where it is written that his mark is on their foreheads. In the last analysis the mood of reverence that should characterize all men's dealings with each other finds its basis here. The demand to treat all human beings as ends in themselves, or the moral imperative that issues in respect for personality, finds its profound inspiration here. To deal with men on any other basis, to treat them as if there were not vibrant and vital in each one the very life of the very God, is the great blasphemy; it is the judgment that is leveled with such relentless severity on modern man. "Thou hast made us for thy self and our souls are restless till they find their rest in thee," says Augustine. Life is like a river.

> Deep River, my home is over Jordan —
> Deep River, I want to cross over into camp ground.
>
> — *Deep River*, 78

Here we are face to face with perhaps the most daring and revolutionary concept known to man: namely, that God is not only the creative mind and spirit at the core of the universe but that He ... is love. There are no completely satisfying ways by which this conclusion may be arrived at by mere or sheer rational reflective processes. This is the great disclosure: that there is at the heart of life a Heart. When such an insight is possessed by the human spirit and possesses the human spirit, a vast and awe-inspiring tranquility irradiates the life. This is the message of the spiritual ["Wade in the Water"]. Do not shrink from moving confidently out into choppy seas. Wade in the water, because God is troubling the water.

> — *Deep River*, 95

The religious experience as I have known it seems to swing wide the door, not merely into Life but into lives. I am confident that my own call to the religious vocation cannot be separated from the slowly emerging disclosure that my religious experience makes it possible for me to experience myself as a human being and thus keep a very real psychological distance between myself and the hostilities of my environment. Through the years it has driven me more and more to seek to make as a normal part of my relations with men the experiencing of them as human beings. When this happens love has essential materials with which to work. And contrary to the general religious teaching, men would not need to stretch themselves out of shape in order to love. On the contrary, a man comes into possession of himself more completely when he is *free* to love another. — *The Luminous Darkness,* 111

PRAYER

In the first place prayer, in the sense in which I am using it, means the *method* by which the individual makes his way to the temple of quiet within his own spirit and the *activity* of his spirit within its walls. Prayer is not only the participation in communication with God in the encounter of religious experience, but it is also the "readying" of the spirit for such communication. It is the total process of quieting down and to that extent must not be separated from meditation. Perhaps, as important as prayer itself, is the "readying" of the spirit for the experience.

In such "readying" a quiet place is very important if not altogether mandatory. In the noise of our times such a place may be impossible to find. One of the great services that the Christian church can render to the community is to provide spells and spaces of quiet for the world-weary men and women whose needs are so desperate...

When one has been thus prepared, a strange thing happens. It is very difficult to put into words. The initiative slips out of one's hands and into the hands of God, the other Principal in the religious experience. The self moves toward God. Such movement seems to have the quality of innate and fundamental stirring. The self does not see itself as being violated, but all of this takes place in a frame of reference that is completely permissive. There is another movement which is at once merged with the movement of the self. God touches the spirit and the will and a wholly new character in terms of dimension enters the experience. In this sense prayer may be regarded as an open-end experience.

Fundamental to the total fact of prayer in the Christian religion is the persuasive affirmation that the God of religious experience is a seeking and a beseeching God. "O Jerusalem, Jerusalem,... how often would I have gathered thy children together, even as a hen gathereth her chickens under her wings, and ye would not." The great parables of "The Lost

Sheep," "The Lost Coin," and "The Prodigal Son" carry the same idea. The discovery of such a fact in one's experience in life is first met in the religious experience itself.   — *The Creative Encounter, 34–35, 37–38*

We must find sources of strength and renewal for our own spirits, lest we perish. There is a widespread recognition of the need for refreshment of the mind and the heart. It is very much in order to make certain concrete suggestions in this regard. First, we must learn to be quiet, to settle down in one spot for a spell. Sometime during each day, everything should stop and the art of being still must be practiced. For some temperaments, it will not be easy because the entire nervous system and body have been geared over the years to activity, to overt and tense functions. Nevertheless, the art of being still must be practiced until development and habit are sure . . .

Such periods may be snatched from the greedy demands of one's day's work. They may be islanded in a sea of other human beings; they may come only at the end of the day, or in the quiet hush of the early morning. We must, each one of us, find his own time and develop his own peculiar art of being quiet. We must lose our fear of rest. There are some of us who keep up our morale (morale has been defined as a belief in one's cause) by being always busy. We have made a fetish of fevered action. We build up our own sense of security by trying to provide a relentless, advantageous contract between ourselves and others by the fevered, intense activities in which we are engaged. Actually, such people are afraid of quiet. Again, most activities become a substitute for the hard-won core of purpose and direction. The time will come when all activities are depressing and heavy, and the dreaded question, "What's the use?" will have to be faced and dealt with. The first step in the discovery of sources of strength and renewal is to develop the art of being still, physical and mental cessation from churning. This is not all, but it is the point at which we begin.
          — *Deep Is the Hunger, 175–76*

To Jesus, God breathed through all that is. The sparrow overcome by sudden death in its evening flight; the lily blossoming on the rocky hillside; the grass of the field and the garden path, the clouds light and burdenless or weighted down with unshed water; the madman in chains or wandering among the barren rocks in the wastelands; the little baby in his mother's arms; the strutting arrogance of the Roman Legion; the brazen queries of the craven tax collector; the children at play or the old men quibbling in the market place; the august Sanhedrin fighting for its life amidst the impudences of Empire; the futile whisper of those who had forgotten Jerusalem; the fear-voiced utterance of the prophets who remembered — to Jesus, God breathed through all that is. To Jesus, God was Creator of life and the living substance; the Living Stream upon which all things moved; the Mind containing time, space, and all their multitudinous offspring. And beyond all these God was Friend and Father.

The time most precious for him was at close of day. This was the time for the long breath, when all the fragments left by the commonplace, when all the little hurts and the big aches could be absorbed, and the mind could be freed of the immediate demand, when voices that had been quieted by the long day's work could once more be heard, when there could be the deep sharing of the innermost secrets and the laying bare of the heart and mind. Yes, the time most precious for him was at close of day.

But there were other times he treasured, "A great while before day," says the Book. The night had been long and wearisome because the day had been full of nibbling annoyances; the high resolve of some winged moment had frenzied, panicked, no longer sure, no longer free, and then had vanished as if it had never been. There was need, the utter urgency, for some fresh assurance, the healing touch of a healing wing. "A great while before day" he found his way to the quiet place in the hills. And prayed. — *The Inward Journey,* 30

BEING HUMAN

The burden of being black and the burden of being white is so heavy that it is rare in our society to experience oneself as a human being. It may be, I do not know, that to experience oneself as a human being is one with experiencing one's fellows as human beings. Precisely what does it mean to experience oneself as a human being? In the first place, it means that the individual must have a sense of kinship to life that transcends and goes beyond the immediate kinship of family or the organic kinship that binds him ethnically or "racially" or nationally. He has to feel that he belongs to his total environment. He has a sense of being an essential part of the structural relationship that exists between him and all other men, and between him, all other men, and the total external environment. As a human being, then, he belongs to life and the whole kingdom of life that includes all that lives and perhaps, also, all that has ever lived. In other words, he sees himself as a part of a continuing, breathing, living existence. To be a human being, then, is to be essentially alive in a living world.   — *The Luminous Darkness, 94*

On one of our visits to Daytona Beach I was eager to show my daughters some of my early haunts. We sauntered down the long street from the church to the riverfront. This had been the path of the procession to the baptismal ceremony in the Halifax River, which I had often described to them. We stopped here and there as I noted the changes that had taken place since that far-off time. At length we passed the playground of one of the white public schools. As soon as Olive and Anne saw the swings, they jumped for joy. "Look, Daddy, let's go over and swing!" This was the inescapable moment of truth that every black parent in America must face sooner or later. What do you say to your child at the crucial moment of primary encounter?

"You can't swing in those swings."

"Why?"

"When we get home and have some cold lemonade I will tell you." When we were home again, and had had our lemonade, Anne pressed for the answer. "We are home now, Daddy. Tell us."

I said, "It is against the law for us to use those swings, even though it is a public school. At present, only white children can play there. But it takes the state legislature, the courts, the sheriffs and policemen, the white churches, the mayors, the banks and businesses, and the majority of white people in the state of Florida — it takes all these to keep two little black girls from swinging in those swings. That is how important you are! Never forget, the estimate of your own importance and self-worth can be judged by how many weapons and how much power people are willing to use to control you and keep you in the place they have assigned to you. You are two very important little girls. Your presence can threaten the entire state of Florida."   — *With Head and Heart, 97*

If being Christian does not demand that all Christians love each other and thereby become deeply engaged in experiencing themselves as human beings, it would seem futile to expect that Christians as Christians would be concerned about the secular community in its gross practices of prejudice and discrimination. If a black Christian and white Christian, in encounter, cannot reach out to each other in mutual realization because of that which they are experiencing in common, then there should be no surprise that the Christian institution has been powerless in the presence of the color bar in society. Rather it has reflected the presence of the color bar within its own institutional life.

On the other hand, if Christians practice brotherhood among Christians, this would be one limited step in the direction of a new order among men. Think of what this would mean. Wherever one Christian met or dealt with another Christian, there would be a socially redemptive encounter. They would be like the Gulf Stream or the Japanese Current tempering and softening the climate in all directions. Indeed the Christian would be a leaven at all levels of the community and in public and private living. Of course, such a situation may lend itself to all kinds of exploitation and betrayals — but the Christian would be one of the bulwarks of integrity in human relations in an immoral society.

— *The Luminous Darkness*, 105

The significance of the religion of Jesus to people who stand with their backs against the wall has always seemed to me to be crucial. It is one emphasis which has been lacking — except where it has been a part of a very unfortunate corruption of the missionary impulse, which is, in a sense, the very heartbeat of the Christian religion. My interest in the problem has been and continues to be both personal and professional. This is the question which individuals and groups who live in our land always under the threat of profound social and psychological displacement face: Why is it that Christianity seems impotent to deal radically, and therefore effectively, with the issues of discrimination and injustice on the basis of race, religion, and national origin? Is this impotency due to a betrayal of the genius of the religion, or is it due to a basic weakness in the religion itself? The question is searching, for the dramatic demonstration of the impotency of Christianity in dealing with the issues is underscored by its apparent inability to cope with it within its own fellowship.

— *Jesus and the Disinherited*, 7–8

JESUS AND THE LOVE-ETHIC

The solution which Jesus found for himself and for Israel, as they faced the hostility of the Greco-Roman world, becomes the word and the work of redemption for all the cast-down people in every generation and in every age. I mean this quite literally. I do not ignore the theological and metaphysical interpretation of the Christian doctrine of salvation. But the underprivileged everywhere have long since abandoned any hope that this type of salvation deals with the crucial issues by which their days are turned into despair without consolation. The basic fact is that Christianity as it was born in the mind of this Jewish teacher and thinker appears as a technique of survival for the oppressed. That it became, through the intervening years, a religion of the powerful and the dominant, used sometimes as an instrument of oppression, must not tempt us into believing that it was thus in the mind and life of Jesus. "In him was life, and the life was the light of men." Wherever his spirit appears, the oppressed gather fresh courage; for he announced the good news that fear, hypocrisy, and hatred, the three hounds of hell that track the trail of the disinherited, need have no dominion over them.

— *Jesus and the Disinherited*, 28–29

Living in a climate of deep insecurity, Jesus, faced with so narrow a margin of civil guarantees, had to find some other basis upon which to establish a sense of well-being. He knew that the goals of religion as he understood them could never be worked out within the then-established order. Deep from within that order he projected a dream, the logic of which would give to all the needful security. There would be room for all, and no man would be a threat to his brother. "The kingdom of God is within." "The Spirit of the Lord is upon me, because he hath anointed me to preach the gospel to the poor."

The basic principles of his way of life cut straight through to the despair of his fellows and found it groundless. By inference he says, "You must abandon your fear of each other and fear only God. You must not indulge in any deception and dishonesty, even to save your lives. Your words must be Yea — Nay; anything else is evil. Hatred is destructive to hated and hater alike. Love your enemy, that you may be children of your Father who is in heaven."   — *Jesus and the Disinherited*, 34–35

The central emphasis of the teaching of Jesus centers upon the relationship of individual to individual, and of all individuals to God. So profound has been the conviction of Christians as to the ultimate significance of his teaching about love that they have rested their case, both for the validity and the supremacy of the Christian religion, at this point. When someone asked Jesus what is the meaning of all the law and the prophets, he gave those tremendous words of Judaism, "Hear, O Israel, the Lord thy God is One, and thou shalt love the Lord thy God with all thy mind, heart, soul, and strength. Thou shalt love thy neighbor as thyself." Jesus rests his case for the ultimate significance of life on the love ethic. Love is the intelligent, kindly but stern expression of kinship of one individual for another, having as its purpose the maintenance and furtherance of life at its highest level. Self-love is the kind of activity having as its purpose the maintenance and furtherance of one's own life at its highest level. All love grows basically out of a qualitative self-regard and is in essence the exercise of that which is spiritual. If we accept the basic proposition that all life is one, arising out of a common center — God, all expressions of love are acts of God. Hate, then, becomes a form of annihilation of self and others; in short — suicide.

—*Deep Is the Hunger*, 108–9

The crucifixion of Jesus Christ reminds us once again of the penalty which any highly organized society exacts of those who violate its laws. The social resistors fall into two general groups — those who resist the established order by doing the things that are in opposition to accepted standards of decency and morality: the criminal, the antisocial, the outlaw; and those who resist the established order because its requirements are too low, too unworthy of the highest and best in man. Each is a menace to organized society and both must be liquidated as disturbers of the peace. Behold then the hill outside of the city of Jerusalem, the criminal and the Holy Man sharing a common judgment, because one rose as high above the conventions of his age as the other descended below. Perhaps it is ever thus. Whenever a Jesus Christ is crucified, there will also be crucified beside him the thief — two symbols of resistance to the established pattern. When Christianity makes central in its doctrine the redemptive significance of the cross, it defines itself ever in terms of the growing edge, the advance guard of the human race, who take the lead in man's long march to the City of God.   —*Deep Is the Hunger*, 31

"My God! My God! Why hast Thou forsaken me!" According to the Gospel of Mark, these are the final words uttered by Jesus before his death. They reveal at once one of the most amazing utterances in the entire literature of religion. Here is one who was convinced that he had followed the will and the leadings of God through all the shifting scenes of his life at a most crucial moment in the development of his own people. He had experimented effectively and conclusively with love and understanding as a way of life; he had spent long hours in prayer and meditation; he had given himself with increasing intensity to a full-orbed understanding of the mind of God, whom he interpreted as Father. The logic of his life had led him to the fateful agony of the cross. He was there keeping his tryst with his Father — but where was his Father? The implication of the cry, which Jesus quotes from one of the Psalms, is that he was surer of God than God was of him. It means also that, in his moment of complete exhaustion, Jesus was making one of the great elemental discoveries about the nature of existence; namely, that often the point at which man becomes most keenly aware of the reality of God is on the lonely height, when he is stripped to the literal substance of himself, with nothing between his soul and an ultimate agony. At such a moment, God is seen as the only reality, and oneness with Him as the only fulfillment. The secondary meaning of this discovery is that the end of life and the meaning of life cannot be summarized in terms of happiness, joy, or even satisfaction. Again and again, we must discover that life may say "No" to our most cherished desires, our high hopes, our great yearning. And we must learn to live with life's "No." This is not only to discover the peace that passeth understanding, which may come when the pain of life is not relieved, but also to know for oneself that God is closest to us when in our agony and frustration, he seems to be farthest away.   — *Deep Is the Hunger,* 161–64

CENTERED IN GOD

My testimony is that life is against all dualism. Life is One. Therefore, a way of life that is worth living must be a way worthy of life itself. Nothing less than that can abide. Always, against all that fragments and shatters and against all things that separate and divide within and without, life labors to meld together into a single harmony. Therefore, failure may remain failure in the context of all our strivings, hatred may continue to be hatred in the social and political arena of the common life, tragedy may continue to yield its anguish and its pain, spreading havoc in the tight circle of our private lives, the dead weight of guilt may not shift its position to make life even for a brief moment more comfortable and endurable, for any of us — all this may be true. Nevertheless, in all these things there is a secret door which leads into the central place, where the Creator of life and the God of the human heart are one and the same. I take my stand for the future and for the generations who follow over the bridges we already have crossed. It is here that the meaning of the hunger of the heart is unified. The Head and the Heart at last inseparable; they are lost in wonder in the One.

— *With Head and Heart*, 269

It may seem to be splitting hairs to say that Destiny is what a man does with his fate. Fate is given; Destiny is won. Fate is the raw materials of experience. They come uninvited and often unanticipated. Destiny is what a man does with these raw materials. A man participates in his fate almost as a spectator or perhaps as a victim; he does not call the tunes. It is important to make clear that this is only an aspect of human experience. To ignore the margin of experience that seems to be unresponsive to any private will or desire is disastrous. To ascribe responsibility for all the things that happen to one to some kind of fate is equally disastrous. It is quite reasonable to say that there are forces in life that are set in motion by something beyond the power of man to comprehend or control. The purpose of such forces, their significance, what it is that they finally mean for human life, only God knows. The point at which they touch us or affect us cannot be fully understood. Why they affect us as they do, what they mean in themselves, we do not know. Sometimes they seem like trial and error, like accidents, like blind erratic power that is without conscience or consciousness, only a gross aliveness. To say that those forces are evil or good presupposes a knowledge of ends which we do not have. The point at which they affect our lives determines whether we call them good or evil. This is a private judgment that we pass upon a segment of our primary contact with the forces of life. Out of this contact we build our destiny. We determine what we shall do with our circumstances. It is here that religion makes one of its most important contributions to life. It is a resource that provides strength, stability, and confidence as one works at one's destiny. It gives assurance of a God who shares in the issue and whose everlasting arms are always there.

> I know not where His islands lift
> The fronded palms in air.
> I only know I cannot drift
> Beyond his love and care.

— *Deep Is the Hunger*, 42–43

The insight of the spiritual ["Jacob's Ladder"] is not only confined to the gothic principle and this sense of tomorrow, which are truly kindred notions, but there is implicit here that each man must face the figure at the top of the ladder. There is a goal. It is some kind of climax to human history. Every man must come to terms with the ultimate problem. How does he relate to something that is final in existence? In one way or another God and the human spirit must come together. Whatever things in life you believe to be true and valid, you and they must sit together in the solitude of your own spirit; and when you do what is on the agenda no form of pretension has any standing there. Even your most vaunting ambition may seem in such a moment to be filthy rags. The one searching item with which you have to deal is, how have you lived your life in the knowledge of your truth? This may not occur for the individual at the time of his dying, or at a moment of crisis, but as you turn the corner today in your own road, suddenly it is upon you. We are all climbing Jacob's ladder, and every round goes higher and higher. All who recognize this as a living part of their experience join with those early destiny-bound singers who marched through all the miseries of slavery confident that they could never be entirely earth-bound.

—*Deep River*, 86–87

There is in every person an inward sea, and in that sea there is an island and on that island there is an altar and standing guard before that altar is the "angel with the flaming sword." Nothing can get by that angel to be placed upon that altar unless it has the mark of your inner authority. Nothing passes "the angel with the flaming sword" to be placed upon your altar unless it be a part of "the fluid area of your consent." This is your crucial link with the Eternal.   —*Meditations of the Heart,* 15

Our Father, we gather ourselves together in all of our available parts to see if somehow there may be made clear for us the meaning of our own lives and the meaning of the journey to which we are committed. We confess our sins, as we wait in Thy presence, those things within us of which we are grossly ashamed, those things within us and those expressions of our lives of which we are scarcely aware until our spirits are sensitized by Thy spirit, things which do violence to Thy purposes and Thy will for us and our world. We want to be better than we are. So often we do not know how. Again and again we are moved by the impulse to be better than we are but we do not quite know how to give way to it, that it might sweep through us with its renewal and its inspiration. We are such divided, tempest-tossed, driven children. If we knew the right words to say, our Father, we would say them, if somehow we could bring our minds and our hearts into focus so that what we mean we say, and what we say we do. If we could do this, it would help us to be whole. Shall we seek to make peace within ourselves by the ordering of our wills in accordance with Thy will, or shall we seek to help those about us whose needs are great and in helping them perhaps find wholeness for ourselves? What shall we do, our Father?

Oh, that we might be unanimous within ourselves, that our total being and our lives might be a tuned instrument in Thy hands, making the kind of music that would calm the distressed, that would heal the broken body and mind, that would bring tenderness to those who feel rejected and outcast. As we wait in Thy presence, our Father, gather us in, that we might be a lung through which Thy spirit may breathe. Is this asking too much? We wait, O God, our Father, we wait.

— The Centering Moment, 84

There must be always remaining in every man's life some place for the singing of angels, some place for that which in itself is breathlessly beautiful and, by an inherent prerogative, throws all the rest of life into a new and creative relatedness, something that gathers up in itself all the freshets of experience from drab and commonplace areas of living and glows in one bright white light of penetrating beauty and meaning — then passes. The commonplace is shot through with new glory; old burdens become lighter; deep and ancient wounds lose much of their old, old hurting. A crown is placed over our heads that for the rest of our lives we are trying to grow tall enough to wear. Despite all the crassness of life, despite all the hardness of life, despite all the harsh discords of life, life is saved by the singing of angels.   *— Deep Is the Hunger, 91–92*

SOURCES

Howard Thurman: Essential Writings, ed. Luther E. Smith, Jr. (Maryknoll, NY: Orbis Books, 2006).

Texts from:

The Centering Moment (New York: Harper & Row, 1969; Richmond, IN: Friends United Press, 1980).

The Creative Encounter (New York: Harper & Row, 1954; Richmond, IN: Friends United Press, 1972).

Deep Is the Hunger (New York: Harper & Row, 1951; Richmond, IN: Friends United Press, 1973).

Deep River (Mills College, CA: Eucalyptus Press, 1945; rev. ed. New York: Harper & Row, 1955; Richmond, IN: Friends United Press, 1975).

The Inward Journey (New York: Harper & Row, 1961; Richmond, IN: Friends United Press, 1971).

Jesus and the Disinherited (Nashville: Abingdon, 1949; Richmond, IN: Friends United Press, 1981; Boston: Beacon Press, 1996).

The Luminous Darkness (New York: Harper & Row, 1965; Richmond, IN: Friends United Press, 1989).

Meditations of the Heart (New York: Harper & Row, 1953; Richmond, IN: Friends United Press, 1976; Boston: Beacon Press, 1999).

With Head and Heart: The Autobiography of Howard Thurman (New York: Harcourt Brace and Co., 1979).

EIGHT

MOTHER MARIA SKOBTSOVA

A Monk in the World

Mother Maria Skobtsova (1891–1945) was born Lisa Pilenko into a prosperous aristocratic family in Russia. In her early life she was a distinguished poet and a committed political activist who married twice, first to a Bolshevik whom she eventually divorced, later to an anti-Bolshevik, from whom she was later separated. During the revolutionary upheaval she served as mayor of her hometown, in the process risking persecution from both the Left and the Right. In 1923, with her three young children, she joined the throng of refugees uprooted by revolution and civil war and made her way to Paris. Soon after her arrival, her youngest daughter, Nastia, died of meningitis. The impact of this loss initiated a profound conversion. She emerged from her mourning with a determination to seek "a more authentic and purified life." She felt she saw a "new road before me and a new meaning in life...to be a mother for all, for all who need maternal care, assistance, or protection."

In Paris she became immersed in social work among the destitute Russian refugees. She sought them out in prisons, hospitals, mental asylums, and in the back streets of the slums. Increasingly, she emphasized the religious dimension of this work, the insight that "each person is the very icon of God incarnate in the world." With this recognition came the need "to accept this awesome revelation of God unconditionally, to venerate the image of God" in her brothers and sisters. If her spirituality focused on any one insight, it was the implications of Christ's double command—to love God with our whole heart, mind, and soul, and to love one's neighbor as oneself.

Her bishop encouraged her to become a nun, but she would take this step only on the assurance that she would be free to develop a new type

105

of monasticism, engaged in the world and marked by the "complete absence of even the subtlest barrier which might separate the heart from the world and its wounds."

In 1932 she made her monastic profession and became Mother Maria. Instead of confining herself to a monastic enclosure she took a lease on a house in Paris, large enough to include a chapel, a soup kitchen, and a shelter for destitute refugees. Her "cell" was a cot in the basement beside the boiler. As she wrote, "At the Last Judgment I shall not be asked whether I was successful in my ascetic exercises, nor how many bows and prostrations I made. Instead I shall be asked, Did I feed the hungry, clothe the naked, visit the sick and the prisoners?"

In 1940 the Germans occupied Paris. Mother Maria might have escaped but she chose to stay, despite the risks. In the context of Nazi racism, her commitment to seek out and revere each person as the icon of God assumed a deliberately subversive meaning. Aside from her usual work of hospitality, she was aided by her chaplain, Father Dimitri Klepinin, in rescuing Jews and other political refugees. Father Dimitri issued false baptismal certificates to scores of Jews. Their efforts, linked to the organized Resistance, continued until they were arrested by the Gestapo in 1943. Father Dimitri and Maria's son Yuri died in Buchenwald. Maria was sent to Ravensbruck concentration camp, where she managed to survive for almost two years under conditions of indescribable cruelty and horror. Though stripped of her religious habit, she remained the nurturing mother, strengthening the faith and courage of her fellow prisoners and helping to keep alive the flame of humanity in the face of every calculated assault.

In becoming a nun Maria had said, "I think service to the world is simply the giving of one's own soul in order to save others." Now in her hunger, illness, and exposure to the elements, she found the ultimate destination of her vocation. In light of the redemptive suffering of Christ she found a meaning to her own suffering. As she wrote in a message smuggled out of the camp, "My state at present is such that I completely accept suffering in the knowledge that this is how things ought to be for me, and if I am to die I see in this a blessing from on high."

She perished in the gas chamber on March 31, 1945, just days before the liberation of the camp by Russian troops.

For many years Mother Maria was viewed with suspicion in Orthodox circles. Her "questionable past," her leftist sympathies, her highly unconventional brand of monasticism, and her outspoken criticism of *various styles of orthodox piety raised eyebrows. She could be scathing in her treatment of "Christian scribes, pharisees, doctors of the law" who set themselves to protecting the church against "authentic Christian fervor," and who, in their zeal for proper liturgy, forgot the essential message of the gospel. "The meaning of the liturgy must be translated into life. It is why Christ came into the world and why he gave us our liturgy."*

But in time her witness has found increasing honor. As Orthodox theologian Olivier Clément commented, "If we love and venerate Mother Maria, it is not in spite of her disorder, her strange views, and her passions. It is precisely these qualities that make her extraordinarily alive among so many bland and pious saints. Unattractive and dirty, strong, thick, and sturdy, yes, she was truly alive in her suffering, her compassion, her passion."

In 2003 she was canonized by the Russian Orthodox Church.

THE EVANGELICAL TYPE

This selection is taken from a long essay entitled "Types of Religious Life," originally written in 1937, though it was only discovered and published in 1996. While it is specifically directed at tendencies within the Russian Orthodox Church, Mother Maria's critique of four "types" of Christianity — the "synodal" (a style of state-sponsored Christianity), ritualist, aesthetical, and ascetical — has a much wider and enduring relevance. Her final section on "the evangelical type" reflects her own ideal. As she notes, what she calls the "evangelical type" does not refer to the modern form of Protestant evangelicalism. It is actually a "Gospel type," an authentic form of Christianity based on an encounter with God in our fellow human beings. It is expressed not only in the liturgy but especially in charity and self-sacrifice.

I will now move on to characterize the evangelical type of spiritual life, which is as eternal as is the proclamation of the Good News, always alive within the bosom of the Church, shining for us in the faces of saints and at times lighting with the reflection of its fire even righteous people outside the Church. (Here one must immediately introduce a clarification so as to prevent well-intentioned or deliberate misinterpretations of the evangelical way of religious life. Obviously it has no relation to the current evangelical sectarianism which has extracted only a selected list of

moral precepts from the Gospel, added to this its own distorted and impoverished doctrine of salvation — about being "born again" — spiced
this up with hatred of the Church, and then proclaimed this peculiar
hodgepodge as a true understanding of Christ's Gospel teaching.) The
evangelical spirit of religious consciousness "blows where it will," but
woe betide those ages and those peoples upon which it does not rest.
And at the same time, blessed are they that walk in its paths — even
those who know it not.

Christification

What is most characteristic of this path? It is a desire to "Christify"
all of life. To a certain degree this notion can be contrasted to that
which is understood not only by the term "churching," but also the
term "christianization." "Churching" is often taken to mean the placing of life within the framework of a certain rhythm of church piety,
the subordination of one's personal life experience to the schedule of
the cycle of divine services, the incorporation of certain specific elements
of "churchliness" into one's way of life, even elements of the Church's
ritual. "Christianization," however, is generally understood as nothing
more than the correction of the bestial cruelty of man's history through
inoculation with a certain dose of Christian morality. And in addition to
this it also includes the preaching of the Gospel to the whole world.

"Christification," however, is based on the words, "It is no longer I
who live, but Christ who lives in me" (Gal. 2:20). The image of God,
the icon of Christ, which truly is my real and actual essence or being, is
the only measure of all things, the only path or way which is given to
me. Each movement of my soul, each approach to God, to other people,
to the world, is determined by the suitability of that act for reflecting the
image of God which is within me.

If I am faced with two paths and I am in doubt, then even if all
human wisdom, experience, and tradition point to one of these, but I
feel that Christ would have followed the other — then all my doubts
should immediately disappear and I should choose to follow Christ in
spite of all the experience, tradition and wisdom that are opposed to it.
But other than the immediate consciousness that Christ is calling me to
a particular path, are there any other objective signs which will tell me
that this doesn't just appear this way to me, that it is not a figment of my
imagination or my emotional feeling? Yes, there are objective indications.

Two commandments

Christ gave us two commandments: to love God and to love our fellow man. Everything else, even the commandments contained in the Beatitudes, is merely an elaboration of these two commandments, which contain within themselves the totality of Christ's "Good News." Furthermore, Christ's earthly life is nothing other than the revelation of the mystery of love of God and love of man. These are, in sum, not only the true but the only measure of all things. And it is remarkable that their truth is found only in the way they are linked together. Love for man alone leads us into the blind alley of an anti-Christian humanism, out of which the only exit is, at times, the rejection of the individual human being and love toward him in the name of all mankind. Love for God without love for man, however, is condemned: "You hypocrite, how can you love God whom you have not seen, if you hate your brother whom you have seen" (1 John 4:20). Their linkage is not simply a combination of two great truths taken from two spiritual worlds. Their linkage is the union of two parts of a single whole.

These two commandments are two aspects of a single truth. Destroy either one of them and you destroy truth as a whole. In fact, if you take away love for man then you destroy man (because by not loving him you reject him, you reduce him to non-being) and no longer have a path toward the knowledge of God. God then becomes truly apophatic, having only negative attributes, and even these can be expressed only in the human language which you have rejected. He becomes inaccessible to your human soul because, in rejecting man, you have also rejected humanity, you have also rejected what is human in your own soul, though your humanity was the image of God within you and your only way to see the Prototype as well. This is to say nothing of the fact that man taught you in his own human language, describing in human words God's truth, nor of the fact that God reveals himself through human concepts. By not loving, by not having contact with humanity we condemn ourselves to a kind of a deaf-mute blindness with respect to the divine as well. In this sense, not only did the Logos-Word-Son of God assume human nature to complete his work of redemption and by this sanctified it once and for all, destining it for deification, but the Word of God, as the "Good News," as the Gospel, as revelation and enlightenment likewise needed to become incarnate in the flesh of insignificant human words. For it is with words that people express their feelings, their doubts, their thoughts, their good deeds and their sins. And in this way human speech, which is the symbol of man's interior life, was likewise sanctified and filled with grace — and through it the whole of man's inner life.

On the other hand, one cannot truly love man without loving God. As a matter of fact, what can we love in man if we do not discern God's image within him? Without that image, on what is such love based? It becomes some kind of peculiar, monstrous, towering egoism in which every "other" becomes only a particular facet of my own self. I love that in the other which is compatible with me, which broadens me, which explains me — and at times simply entertains and charms me. If, however, this is not the case, if indeed there is desire for a selfless but non-religious love toward man, then it will move inevitably from a specific person of flesh and blood and turn toward the abstract man, toward humanity, even to the idea of humanity, and will almost always result in the sacrifice of the concrete individual upon the altar of this abstract idea — the common good, an earthly paradise, etc.

Two kinds of love

In this world there are two kinds of love: one that takes and one that gives. This is common to all types of love — not only love for man. One can love a friend, one's family, children, scholarship, art, the motherland, one's own ideas, oneself — and even God — from either of these two points of view. Even those forms of love that by common consent are the highest can exhibit this dual character.

Take, for example, maternal love. A mother can often forget herself, sacrifice herself for her children. Yet this does not as yet warrant recognition as Christian love for her children. One needs to ask the question: what is it that she loves in them? She may love her own reflection, her second youth, an expansion of her own "I" into other "I"s which become separated from the rest of the world as "we." She may love in them her own flesh that she sees in them, the traits of her own character, the reflections of her own tastes, the continuation of her family. Then it becomes unclear where is the fundamental difference between an egotistical love of self and a seemingly sacrificial love of one's children, between "I" and "we." All this amounts to a passionate love of one's own which blinds one's vision, forcing one to ignore the rest of the world — what is not one's own.

Such a mother will imagine that the merit of her own child is not comparable with the merit of other children, that his mishaps and illnesses are more severe than those of others, and, finally, that at times the well-being and success of other children can be sacrificed for the sake of the well-being and success of her own. She will think that the whole world (herself included) is called to serve her child, to feed him, quench his thirst, train him, make smooth all paths before him, deflect all obstacles and all rivals. This is a kind of passion-filled maternal love.

Only that maternal love is truly Christian which sees in the child a true image of God, which is inherent not only in him but in all people, but given to her in trust, as her responsibility, as something she must develop and strengthen in him in preparation for the unavoidable life of sacrifice along the Christian path, for that cross-bearing challenge which faces every Christian. Only such a mother loves her child with truly Christian love. With this kind of love she will be more aware of other children's misfortunes, she will be more attentive toward them when they are neglected. As the result of the presence of Christian love in her heart her relationship with the rest of humanity will be a relationship in Christ. This is, of course, a very poignant example.

There can be no doubt but that love for anything that exists is divided into these two types. One may passionately love one's mother-land, working to make sure that it develops gloriously and victoriously, overcoming and destroying all its enemies. Or one can love it in a Christian manner, working to see that the face of Christ's truth is revealed more and more clearly within it. One can passionately love knowledge and art, seeking to express oneself, to flaunt oneself in them. Or one can love them while remaining conscious of one's service through them, of one's responsibility for the exercise of God's gifts in these spheres.

One can also love the idea of one's own life simply because it is one's own — and enviously and jealously set it over against all other ideas. Or one can see in it too a gift granted to one by God for the service of his eternal truth during the time of one's path on earth. One can love life itself both passionately and sacrificially. One can even relate to death in two different ways. And one can direct two kinds of love toward God. One of these will look on him as the heavenly protector of "my" or "our" earthly passions and desires. Another kind of love, however, will humbly and sacrificially offer one's tiny human soul into his hands. And apart from their name — love — and apart from their outward appearance, these two forms of love will have nothing in common.

True asceticism

In the light of such Christian love, what should man's ascetic effort be? What is that true asceticism whose existence is inescapably presupposed by the very presence of spiritual life? Its criterion is self-denying love for God and for one's fellow man. But an asceticism which puts one's own soul at the center of everything, which looks for its salvation, fencing it off from the world, and within its own narrow limits comes close to spiritual self-centeredness and a fear of dissipating, of wasting one's energies, even though it be through love — this is not Christian asceticism.

What is the criterion that can be used to define and measure the various pathways of human life? What are their prototypes, their primary symbols, their boundaries? It is the path of Godmanhood, Christ's path upon earth. The Word became flesh, God became incarnate, born in a stable in Bethlehem. This alone should be fully sufficient for us to speak of the limitless, sacrificial, self-abnegating and self-humbling love of Christ. Everything else is present in this. The Son of Man lowered the whole of himself — the whole of his divinity, his whole divine nature and his whole divine hypostasis — beneath the vaults of that cave in Bethlehem. There are not two Gods, nor are there two Christs: one who abides in blessedness within the bosom of the Holy Trinity and another who took on the form of a servant. The Only-begotten Son of God, the Logos, has become Man, lowering himself to the level of mankind. The path of his later life — the preaching, the miracles, the prophesies, the healings, the enduring of hunger and thirst, right through his trial before Pilate, the way of the cross and on to Golgotha and death — all this is the path of his humiliated humanity, and together with him the path of God's condescension to humanity.

Self-denying love

What was Christ's love like? Did it withhold anything? Did it observe or measure its own spiritual gifts? What did it regret? Where was it ever stingy? Christ's humanity was spit upon, struck, crucified. Christ's divinity was incarnate fully and to the end in his spit-upon, battered, humiliated and crucified humanity. The Cross — an instrument of shameful death — has become for the world a symbol of self-denying love. And at no time nor place — neither from Bethlehem to Golgotha, neither in sermons nor parables, nor in the miracles he performed — did Christ ever give any occasion to think that he did not sacrifice himself wholly and entirely for the salvation of the world, that there was in him something held back, some "holy of holies" which he did not want to offer or should not have offered.

He offered his own "holy of holies," his own divinity, for the sins of the world, and this is precisely wherein lies his divine and perfect love in all its fullness. This is the only conclusion we can come to from the whole of Christ's earthly ministry. But can it be that the power of divine love is such because God, though offering himself, still remains God, that is, does not empty himself, does not perish in this dreadful sacrificial self-emptying? Human love cannot be completely defined in terms of the laws of divine love, because along this path a man can lay himself waste and lose sight of what is essential: the salvation of his soul.

But here one need only pay attention to what Christ taught us. He said: "If any man would come after me, let him deny himself, and take up his cross." Self-denial is of the essence, and without it no one can follow him, without it there is no Christianity. Keep nothing for yourself. Lay aside not only material wealth but spiritual wealth as well, changing everything into Christ's love, taking it up as your cross. He also spoke — not about himself and not about his perfect love, but about the love which human imperfection can assume — "Greater love has no man than he who lays down his soul for his friends" (John 15:13). How miserly and greedy it is to understand the word "soul" here as "life." Christ is speaking here precisely about the soul, about surrendering one's inner world, about utter and unconditional self-sacrifice as the supreme example of the love that is obligatory for Christians. Here again there is no room for looking after one's own spiritual treasures. Here everything is given up.

Spiritual poverty

Christ's disciples followed in his path. This is made quite clear in an almost paradoxical expression of the Apostle Paul: "I could wish that I myself were accursed and cut off from Christ for the sake of my brethren" (Rom. 9:3). And he said this, having stated: "It is no longer I who live, but Christ who lives in me" (Gal. 2:20). For him such an estrangement from Christ is an estrangement from life not only in the transient, worldly sense of the word, but from the eternal and incorruptible life of the age to come.

These examples suffice to let us know where Christianity leads us. Here love truly does not seek its own, even if this be the salvation of one's own soul. Such love takes everything from us, deprives us of everything, almost as if it were devastating us. And where does it lead? To spiritual poverty. In the Beatitudes we are promised blessedness in return for being poor in spirit. This precept is so far removed from human understanding that some people attempt to read the word "spirit" as a later interpolation and explain these words as a call for material poverty and a rejection of earthly riches, while others almost slip into fanaticism, taking this as a call for intellectual poverty, the rejection of thought and of any kind of intellectual content. Yet how simply and clearly these words can be interpreted in the context of other evangelical texts. The person who is poor in spirit is the one who lays down his soul for his friends, offering this spirit out of love, not withholding his spiritual treasures.

Here the spiritual significance of the monastic vow of nonpossession becomes evident. Of course it does not refer just to material nonpossession or a basic absence of avarice. Here it is a question of spiritual nonpossession.

What is the opposite of this? What vices correspond to the virtue of nonpossession? There are two of them, and in real life they are frequently confused: stinginess and greed. One can be greedy but at the same time not be stingy, and even extravagant. One can also be stingy but not have a greedy desire to possess what is not one's own. Both are equally unacceptable. And if it is unacceptable in the material world, it is even less acceptable in the spiritual realm.

Nonpossession teaches us not only that we should not greedily seek advantage for our soul, but that we must not be stingy with our soul, that we should squander our soul in love, that we should achieve spiritual nakedness, that spiritually we should be stripped bare. There should be nothing so sacred or valuable that we would not be ready to give it up in the name of Christ's love to those who have need of it.

Spiritual nonpossession is the way of the holy fool. It is folly, foolishness in Christ. It is the opposite of the wisdom of this age. It is the blessedness of those who are poor in spirit. It is the outer limit of love, the sacrifice of one's own soul. It is separation from Christ in the name of one's brothers. It is the denial of oneself. And this is the true Christian path which is taught us by every word and every phrase of the Gospels.

Why is it that the wisdom of this world not only opposes this commandment of Christ but simply fails to understand it? Because the world has at all times lived by accommodating itself to the laws of material nature and is inclined to carry these laws over into the realm of spiritual nature. According to the laws of matter, I must accept that if I give away a piece of bread, then I became poorer by one piece of bread. If I give away a certain sum of money, then I have reduced my funds by that amount. Extending this law, the world thinks that if I give my love, I am impoverished by that amount of love, and if I give up my soul, then I am utterly ruined, for there is nothing left of me to save.

In this area, however, the laws of spiritual life are the exact opposite of the laws of the material world. According to spiritual law, every spiritual treasure given away not only returns to the giver like a whole and unbroken ruble given to a beggar, but it grows and becomes more valuable. He who gives, acquires, and he who becomes poor, becomes rich. We give away our human riches and in return we receive much greater gifts from God, while he who gives away his human soul, receives in return eternal bliss, the divine gift of possessing the Kingdom of heaven. How does he receive that gift? By absenting himself from Christ in an act of the uttermost self-renunciation and love, he offers himself to others. If this is indeed an act of Christian love, if this self-renunciation is genuine, then he meets Christ himself face to face in the one to whom he offers himself. And in communion with him he communes with Christ himself. That from which he absented himself he obtains anew, in love, and in a true communion with God. Thus the mystery of union with man becomes the mystery of union with God. What was given away returns, for the love which is poured out never diminishes the source of that love, for the source of love in our hearts is Love itself. It is Christ.

We are not speaking here about good deeds, nor about that love which measures and parcels out its various possibilities, which gives away the interest but keeps hold of the capital. Here we are speaking about a genuine draining of self, in partial imitation of Christ's self-emptying of himself when he became incarnate in mankind. In the same way we must empty ourselves completely, becoming incarnate, so to speak, in another human soul, offering to it the full strength of the divine image which is contained within ourselves.

It was this — and only this — which was rejected by the wisdom of this world, as being a kind of violation of its laws. It was this that made the Cross a symbol of divine love: foolishness for the Greeks and a stumbling block for the Jews, though for us it is the only path to salvation. There is not, nor can there be, any doubt but that in giving ourselves to another in love — to the poor, the sick, the prisoner — we will encounter in him Christ himself, face to face. He told us about this himself when he spoke of the Last Judgment: how he will call some to eternal life because they showed him love in the person of each unfortunate and miserable individual, while others he will send away from himself because their hearts were without love, because they did not help him in the person of his suffering human brethren in whom he revealed himself to them. If we harbor doubts about this on the basis of our unsuccessful everyday experience, then we ourselves are the only reason for these doubts: our loveless hearts, our stingy souls, our ineffective will, our lack of faith in Christ's help. One must really be a fool for Christ in order to travel this path to its end — and at its end, again and again, encounter Christ. This alone is our all-consuming Christian calling.

The Eucharist

And this, I believe, is the evangelical way of piety. It would be incorrect, however, to think that this has been revealed to us once and for all in the four Gospels and clarified in the Epistles. It is continually being revealed and is a constant presence in the world. It is also continually being accomplished in the world, and the form of its accomplishment is the Eucharist, the Church's most valuable treasure, its primary activity in the world. The Eucharist is the mystery of sacrificial love. Therein lies its whole meaning, all its symbolism, all its power. In it Christ again and again is voluntarily slain for the sins of the world. Again and again the sins of the world are raised by him upon the Cross. And he gives himself — his Body and Blood — for the salvation of the world. By offering himself as food for the world, by giving to the world communion in his Body and Blood, Christ not only saves the world by his sacrifice, but makes each person himself a "christ," and unites him to his own self-sacrificing love for the world. He takes flesh from the world, he deifies this human flesh, he gives it up for the salvation of the world and then unites the world again to this sacrificed flesh — both for its salvation and for its participation in this sacrificial offering. Along with himself — in himself — Christ offers the world as well as a sacrifice for the expiation of our sins, as if demanding from the world this sacrifice of love as the only path toward union with him, that is, for salvation. He raises the world as well upon the Cross, making it a participant in his death and in his glory.

How profound is the resonance of these words of the Eucharist: "Thine own of thine own we offer unto thee, on behalf of all and for all." The Eucharist here is the Gospel in action. It is the eternally existing and eternally accomplished sacrifice of Christ and of Christ-like

human beings for the sins of the world. Through it earthly flesh is deified and having been deified enters into communion again with earthly
flesh. In this sense the Eucharist is true communion with the divine. And
is it not strange that in it the path to communion with the divine is so
closely bound up with our communion with each other. It assumes consent to the exclamation: "Let us love one another, that with one mind
we may confess Father, Son and Holy Spirit: the Trinity, one in essence
and undivided."

The Eucharist needs the flesh of this world as the "matter" of the mystery. It reveals to us Christ's sacrifice as a sacrifice on behalf of mankind,
that is, as his union with mankind. It makes us into "christs," repeating
again and again the great mystery of God meeting man, again and again
making God incarnate in human flesh. And all this is accomplished in
the name of sacrificial love for mankind.

But if at the center of the Church's life there is this sacrificial, self-
giving eucharistic love, then where are the Church's boundaries, where
is the periphery of this center? Here it is possible to speak of the whole of
Christianity as an eternal offering of the Divine Liturgy beyond church
walls. What does this mean? It means that we must offer the bloodless
sacrifice, the sacrifice of self-surrendering love not only in a specific place,
upon the altar of a particular temple; the whole world becomes the single
altar of a single temple, and for this universal Liturgy we must offer our
hearts, like bread and wine, in order that they may be transubstantiated
into Christ's love, that he may be born in them, that they may become
"God-manly" hearts, and that he may give these hearts of ours as food
for the world, that he may bring the whole world into communion with
these hearts of ours that have been offered up, so that in this way we
may be one with him, not so that we should live anew but so that Christ
should live in us, becoming incarnate in our flesh, offering our flesh upon
the Cross of Golgotha, resurrecting our flesh, offering it as a sacrifice of
love for the sins of the world, receiving it from us as a sacrifice of love
to himself. Then truly in all ways Christ will be in all.

Communion with God and man

Here we see the measurelessness of Christian love. Here is the only path
toward becoming Christ, the only path which the Gospel reveals to us.
What does all this mean in a worldly, concrete sense? How can this be
manifested in each human encounter, so that each encounter may be a
real and genuine communion with God through communion with man?

It implies that each time one must give up one's soul to Christ in order that he may offer it as a sacrifice for the salvation of that particular individual. It means uniting oneself with that person in the sacrifice of Christ, in flesh of Christ. This is the only injunction we have received through Christ's preaching of the Gospel, corroborated each day in the celebration of the Eucharist. Such is the only true path a Christian can follow. In the light of this path all others grow dim and hazy. One must not, however, judge those who follow other conventional, non-sacrificial paths, paths which do not require that one offer up oneself, paths which do not reveal the whole mystery of love. Nor, on the other hand, is it permitted to be silent about them. Perhaps in the past it was possible, but not today.

Such terrible times are coming. The world is so exhausted from its scabs and its sores. It so cries out to Christianity in the secret depths of its soul. But at the same time it is so far removed from Christianity that Christianity cannot, should not even dare to show a distorted, diminished, darkened image of itself. Christianity should singe the world with the fire of Christian love. Christianity should ascend the Cross on behalf of the world. It should incarnate Christ himself in the world. Even if this Cross, eternally raised again and again on high, be foolishness for our new Greeks and a stumbling block for our new Jews, for us it will still be "the power of God and the wisdom of God" (1 Cor. 1:24).

We who are called to be poor in spirit, to be fools for Christ, who are called to persecution and abuse — we know that this is the only calling given to us by the persecuted, abused, disdained and humiliated Christ. And we not only believe in the Promised Land and the blessedness to come: now, at this very moment, in the midst of this cheerless and despairing world, we already taste this blessedness whenever, with God's help and at God's command, we deny ourselves, whenever we have the strength to offer our soul for our neighbors, whenever in love we do not seek our own ends.

SOURCE

Excerpted from "Types of Religious Life," in *Mother Maria Skobtsova: Essential Writings* (Maryknoll, NY: Orbis Books, 2003). This translation, by Fr. Alvian Smirensky and Elisabeth Obolensky, first appeared in *Sourozh,* the diocesan journal of the Russian Orthodox Church in Britain.

NINE

DOM HELDER CAMARA
Mystic and Prophet

Dom Helder Camara (1909–1999), the courageous and prophetic arch-bishop of Recife, Brazil, was one of the great apostles of Christian nonviolence in the twentieth century. He embodied what became known as the church's "preferential option for the poor," and defined through his actions the intimate relationship between love and justice.

In this role he traveled a considerable distance from his early years as a priest. At the time of his ordination in 1931 the church's prin-cipal concerns were combating communism and religious indifference. Camara joined a conservative political movement, the Integralist Party, which was inspired by Italian fascism. Their motto was "God, Country, Family." It was not long, however, before he broke with this movement. While engaged in pastoral work in Rio de Janeiro he had become in-creasingly affected by the condition of the poor, the inhabitants of Rio's squalid slums, or favelas. Endeavoring to relate the message of the gospel to their sufferings, he underwent a steady and radical conversion until he reached the point where he himself was labeled a dangerous subversive. As he later noted, "When I care for the poor they call me a saint; when I ask why so many people are poor they call me a communist."

Camara was named a bishop in 1952. He was instrumental in found-ing the National Conference of Brazilian Bishops, the first such body of its kind in Latin America. He himself served as its secretary general for twelve years, and under his leadership this body became a vigorous advocate for the poor and a defender of human rights. As an auxiliary bishop of Rio, Camara organized many social services for the poor, but he gradually came to the conclusion that charity was not enough. What was needed was social justice. This in turn required empowering the poor

119

to be agents of social transformation. Thus, Camara began to put more emphasis on grassroots education or "conscientization," as the Brazilian educator Paulo Freire called it.

Camara attended the Second Vatican Council, where he emerged as a spokesman for the bishops from the "underdeveloped" world. Picking up on a phrase from Pope John XXIII, he called on the church to recover its true identity and vocation as a "church of the poor."

In 1964 Camara was named archbishop of Recife and Olinda in the impoverished northeast region of Brazil. His installation virtually coincided with a brutal military coup. Camara immediately stepped forward as a champion of democracy and human rights, a role that earned him the nickname "the red bishop." He matched his words with a new style of episcopal leadership. Instead of a pectoral cross of gold or silver, he wore a simple wooden cross. He opened the seminary to women and lay people for theological study and pastoral training. He moved out of the bishop's palace and lived in a humble house, where his door was always open to anyone who sought him.

Among those who once knocked on his door was a hired assassin. When Dom Helder answered the door and identified himself, the man was so undone by the sight of the frail and diminutive bishop that he abandoned his deadly mission. "I can't kill you," he said. "You are one of the Lord's."

This was not the only time Dom Helder was close to death. His house was sprayed with machine-gun fire. The diocesan offices were repeatedly ransacked. For thirteen years he was banned by the military government from speaking in public, and the newspapers were not even permitted to mention his name. Though his life was spared, he endured a more painful fate — to see his friends and colleagues repeatedly imprisoned, tortured, or killed simply because of their association with him.

The fear of this single pastor seemed almost comical in light of his appearance. At just over five feet tall, and weighing no more than 120 pounds in his traditional soutane, Dom Helder hardly looked the part of a dangerous revolutionary. Yet there was no mistaking his passion and strength of will when it came to defending the poor.

For all his anger in the face of injustice, Dom Helder conveyed a deep spirit of interior peace and even joy. He rose every night at two to pray and recite his breviary. His day formally began with Mass at six. Thus rooted in prayer, he was able in each situation or encounter to discern the *face of God. Within the body of this frail old man, there beat the heart of a mystic. Like St. Francis, he had the habit of speaking to animals and even inanimate objects that crossed his path. Often he interrupted a conversation to wave at a flock of passing birds or even an airplane overhead. "I love everybody!" he liked to exclaim with arms upraised. And everybody and everything he encountered received his blessing.*

One of his constant themes was the importance of what he called the "Abrahamic minority," the small community of those in each generation who keep hope alive and who are willing to risk their security and comfort to seek the "promised land." The term also referred to the patriarch's effort to bargain with God for the survival of Sodom. Would God not spare the city for the sake of 50 just men? 20? 10? As he wrote, "Whoever hopes against hope, like Abraham, and decides to work, even sacrifice for a more just and humane world, belongs to these Abrahamic minorities."

For such scattered minorities, whether in Brazil or around the world, Dom Helder became an inspiration — a universal bishop to the poor, a friend and pastor to all who struggled for peace and justice. When he retired as archbishop of Recife in 1985, his conservative successor reversed nearly all of his pastoral initiatives. Thus, he lived on to see much of his work swept away.

And yet Dom Helder's witness and spirituality have left an indelible mark on the church. The selections that follow reflect his distinctive merging of the mystical and the political, showing how an intimate experience of God can lead to a radical engagement with the world and its problems.

ABRAHAMIC FAITH

God thinks of all men but calls some to special work. He drives these to take a leap in the dark, to set out. He tries them by fearful hardships. But he supports and encourages them. He gives them the fine and dangerous mission to act as his instruments. He entrusts them with the task of being present discreetly when decisive decisions are made. He sends them out on the road to draw others to them, many others. He expects them to bear witness in the hour of trial.

Abraham was the first to be thus called by God. He did not delay for a moment. He set out. He faced hardships. He learned to his cost how to arouse his brothers in the name of God. To call. To encourage. To start moving...

Did Abraham receive great gifts? He gave a faithful return, the best he could. He served.   —DF, 8–9

We are told that Abraham and other patriarchs heard the voice of God. Can we also hear the Lord's call? Isn't it pretentious to say this? Dangerously presumptuous?

We live in a world where millions of our fellow men live in inhuman conditions, practically in slavery. If we are not deaf we hear the cries of the oppressed. Their cries are the voice of God.

We who live in rich countries where there are always pockets of underdevelopment and wretchedness, hear if we want to hear, the unvoiced demands of those who have no voice and no hope. The pleas of those who have no voice and no hope are the voice of God.

Anyone who has become aware of the injustices caused by the unfair division of wealth, must, if he has a heart, listen to the silent or violent protests of the poor. The protests of the poor are the voice of God...

Are we so deaf that we do not hear a loving God warning us that humanity is in danger of committing suicide? Are we so selfish that we do not hear the just God demanding that we do all we can to stop injustice suffocating the world and driving it to war? Are we so alienated that we can worship God at our ease in luxurious temples which are often empty in spite of all their liturgical pomp, and fail to see, hear, and serve God where he is present and where he requires our presence, among mankind, the poor, the oppressed, the victims of injustices in which we ourselves are often involved?

It is not difficult to hear God's call today in the world about us. It is difficult to do more than offer an emotional response, sorrow, and regret. It is even more difficult to give up our comfort, break with old habits, let ourselves be moved by grace and change our life, be converted.

                                                                —DF, 16–17

Setting out is first of all getting out of ourselves. Breaking through the shell of selfishness hardening us within our own ego.

To stop revolving round ourselves as if were the center of everything.

Refusing to be ringed in by the problems of our own small world. However important these may be humanity is more important and our task is to serve humanity.

Setting out is not covering miles of land or sea, or traveling faster than the speed of sound. It is first and foremost opening ourselves to other people, trying to get to know them, going out to meet them...

It is possible to travel alone. But the good traveler knows that the journey is human life and life needs company. "Companion" means, etymologically, he who eats the same bread. Happy are they who feel they are always on the road and that every man they meet is their chosen companion. The good traveler takes care of his weary companions. He guesses when they lose heart. He takes them as he finds them, listens to them. Intelligently, gently, above all lovingly, he encourages them to go on and recover their joy in the journey.

To travel for the sake of traveling is not the true journey. We must seek a goal, envisage an end to the journey, an arrival.

But there are journeys and journeys. For the Abrahamic minorities, setting out means to get moving and help many others get moving to make the world juster and more human.   — *DF*, 20–21

We must have no illusions. We must not be naïve. If we listen to the voice of God, we make our choice, get out of ourselves and fight nonviolently for a better world. We must not expect to find it easy; we shall not walk on roses, people will not throng to hear us and applaud, and we shall not always be aware of divine protection. If we are to be pilgrims for justice and peace, we must expect the desert...

Our weariness spreads from the body to the soul, which is worse than any bodily exhaustion.

We feel the desert round us as far as our eyes can see. Soft sand which we sink in up to our knees. Blinding and burning sand storms, which hurt our face, get in our eyes and ears...

We reach the limit of endurance, desert all about us, desert within. We feel that the Father himself has abandoned us. "Why hast thou forsaken me?"...

We must not trust in our own strength, we must not give way to bitterness, we must stay humble knowing that we are in the hands of God. We must want only to share in the making of a better world. Then we shall not lose our courage or our hope. We shall feel the invisible protection of God our Father.   — *DF*, 24–25

The more we have to lose, the more weighty becomes our decision to respond to God's call, and the more fiercely and subtly we resist. "It's

not sensible to carry what may be just an impulse too far." "The structures which have been built up over centuries cannot and should not be
changed in a few hours or even days, weeks, or years..."

We must go beyond "aid" or "charity" and demand justice which will
bring peace. Many people falter at this point. He who asks the powerful
to give aid to the poor, or helps the poor himself by being imprudent
enough, or bold enough, to mention these or those rights or demands
this or that justice, is regarded as a splendid man, a saint. But he who
chooses to demand justice generally, seeking to changes structures that
reduce millions of God's children to slavery, must expect his words to
be distorted, to be libeled and slandered, viewed with disfavor by governments, perhaps imprisoned, tortured, killed... But this is the eighth
beatitude: "Blessed are you when men revile you and persecute you and
utter all kinds of evil against you falsely on my account. Rejoice and
be glad for your reward is great in heaven, for so many persecuted the
prophets who were before you."   — DF, 46–47

If you feel you belong in spirit to the family of Abraham do not wait for
permission to act. Don't wait for official action or new laws. The family
of Abraham is more a spirit than an institution, more a lifestyle than an
organization. It requires the minimum of structures and refers merely to
several general principles.

The minimum of structures: anyone who feel he belongs to the family
of Abraham should not remain alone. Make an effort to find someone,
near at hand, or further away, who already belongs to this family, or
who could belong. Make contact. The essential thing is to get out of
isolation. There are no rules about the formation of groups... You are
brothers meeting to help each other find encouragement and develop the
necessary faith, hope, and love...

Choosing the way of moral pressure is not choosing the easy way
out. We are replacing the force of arms by moral force, the violence of
the truth. We must believe that love can strengthen the courage and the
numbers of these Abrahamic minorities who want justice but who refuse
to answer violence with violence.

Love will find the way to rouse and organize these minorities in all
human groups.

Love will find the best way to unite without uniformity these various
nonviolent movements so that they can help each other.

Love will help them to decide firmly that the goal is not superficial reform but the transformation of inhuman structures, to find methods which although they are nonviolent are useful and effective in bringing about this transformation. —*DF,* 54, 58, 60

Question: You see so much misery, so many injustices ... How can you still be so smiling, joyous, optimistic?

I shall try to tell you. You remember that God was willing to let Sodom live, have a future, have salvation, if Abraham could find there not fifty, not forty, not thirty, but only ten just persons. This is the same God who looks at the world today, just as always. Suffering, injustice, and selfishness offend God. But God knows the weaknesses and strengths of all creatures. God respects them and loves them. God sent the Son among them, and left them the Spirit. God knows that there are far more than ten just persons! How could I not share the trust that God places in God's daughters and sons, my sisters and brothers?

In my country and everywhere I go it is true that I encounter misery, misfortune, violence, hate. But it is also true that I encounter numberless crowds of men and women, young people of all ages, who refuse to accept this situation, who thirst for justice and peace, who are ready for anything when it comes to building a world where people can breathe, a world of brothers and sisters. This gives me enormous courage.

—*QL,* 11

MEETING CHRIST

[Every night] I try to recover unity with Christ. And with him I relive the meetings of the past day. I think, for instance, about the mother who told me about the problems she has with her husband, with her children, and how hard she finds it to feed them. And, through this very real mother whom I know by name, I think about all the mothers throughout the world, throughout the ages; the poor ones, the rich ones, the happy ones, the unhappy ones. Or I think about the man I saw working in the streets, emptying dustbins. I had caught his eye. He didn't dare offer me his hand. I virtually had to force him: "Work isn't what soils our hands, friend. No hand was ever soiled by work. Self-centeredness is what soils them." This man, Francisco or Antonio as he may be, reminds me of working men throughout the world throughout the ages. Then I say to Christ our brother, "Lord, two thousand years after your death injustices

are growing worse and worse." Reviewing the day like this, I find time
passes very quickly.   — *TTG*, 6–7

Christ came for all people of all times. But he found the best way of
being present everywhere was to choose one particular spot in the world,
a certain culture, a specific language. This is an important lesson for all
those of us who are charged with perpetuating the living presence of
Christ. We haven't been created to exist in a vacuum. Oh no! We've been
created to be incarnate in some corner of the world, in which we've been
put or to which we are led by the will of God.

Here in Brazil I meet missionaries from almost every country in
the world: priests, religious, members of the laity. They come to us
in the spirit of the incarnation. They assume our culture, they speak
our language. They merge so thoroughly with our people, they become
our brothers and sisters. They take on all our own problems. Not to
solve them, but to encourage us to do so. Through them, through all
of us together, the incarnation goes on, and so does the redemption.
                                                                        — *TTG*, 7–8

When I think of all [these] different worlds united in the human creature
here on earth, I feel myself to be brother to each of them. Joyfully I lend
my voice to the stones, the trees, the animals in my street and those in the
forest. And I say: Perhaps you don't know how to talk or think. Perhaps
you don't know there's a Creator. So I shall speak for you. I'm lending
you my voice.

By the same token I think, if there are millions of creatures that
perhaps have never heard the name of Christ, yet Christ is with them
nonetheless. Christ is everywhere, with God's entire creation, and not
merely with those who know him. The only difference between Christians who do know Christ and the others who don't is that we have
greater responsibilities.   — *TTG*, 9–10

On Mary Magdalene meeting the risen Lord

I like to think of Mary Magdalene as the apostle to the apostles...But
knowing how much Mary Magdalene loved the Lord, it's hard to understand why she couldn't recognize him right away. She actually thought
he was the gardener. It was the same too with the disciples who met the
risen Christ on the way to Emmaus. They had lived with the Lord for
three years. When you love somebody, you can recognize them by their

voice or even by the way they walk. But no, they walked and talked with him and still they couldn't recognize him. Until he shared the loaf with them.

I was thinking about this one day when someone knocked on my door. It was a poor man. He had interrupted my meditation on the disciples at Emmaus: how was it they hadn't been able to recognize Christ? To get rid of the fellow as quickly as I could, I gave him a little cash, a smile and goodbye. But the moment the door was shut, I realized: "You've behaved exactly like the disciples at Emmaus. The Lord Jesus knocked on your door, he spoke to you, and you couldn't get rid of the living Christ fast enough to return to your thoughts on the blindness of your brothers, the disciples of Emmaus."

Often too, when reading the story of the disciples at Emmaus, I think of the responsibility we owe to those who are perhaps at the gates of despair. Our door, on which they knock, for them it may be the last. They ask and they listen perhaps for the last time. It's important to have time to spare for people who, like the disciples at Emmaus, have reached the gates of despair.

Oh, what a grace, Lord, it would be, to be transparent to the living Christ within us! And to remember that the disciples of Emmaus recognized Christ the moment he broke the loaf. When I say Mass and break the bread, I always think of the Lord's ingenuity in this. — *TTG*, 145–46

PROPHECY

I think the word "prophet" is used in an over-specialized sense, as though the Lord only charged a small number of people with the responsibility of being one. Whereas we all as members of the Church have a prophetic mission. The whole Church is called to be prophetic, that is to say, to proclaim the word of the Lord and also to lend the Lord's voice to those who have no voice, to do exactly what Christ, when reading from Isaiah, declared his own personal mission to be: "The spirit of the Lord is on me. He has sent me to bring the good news to the poor, to open their eyes and set them free." This has always been the Church's mission.

As with prophecy, I always say, so with holiness; although admittedly, in the words of the hymn, "the Lord alone is holy," essentially holy. But by baptism, by sanctifying grace, we are made sharers in the Lord's holiness. This isn't a favor reserved for the few. It's a gift and an obligation for us all. And being holy doesn't mean having visions or working miracles. It means living by sanctifying grace, constantly mindful that we carry Christ within us and that we walk within God.

One day I was taking [communion] to an invalid. This was in Rio de Janeiro. The tram was packed. I kept my feet as best I could. I was carrying Christ. On the tram there was a woman with her children. I looked at them; it was Christ looking at them. There were workmen, a very pretty girl; it was Christ looking at them. Eventually I reached the sick man's house. After hearing his confession, I gave him the host, the Eucharistic Christ. And then, for a few seconds, I was tempted to think, "How dreary the return journey's going to be! I shall be all on my own..." But then I thought, "No, you won't! True, you won't be carrying Christ in the Eucharist any more, but the Lord will still be there, ever present."

So being holy isn't an exceptional privilege. How can we get angry if the God of goodness is within us? How can we be jealous if the Lord is with us? How can we be selfish if the God of compassion and sharing is there?

So it is with prophecy. Being a prophet isn't a mission confined to the few. The Spirit of God is on us. Not only on you, or him, or her, or me, but all of us.   — TTG, 43–44

We are never completely converted. We have to keep on converting ourselves every day.

One day some nuns invited me to say Mass to mark the sixtieth year of profession of one of them, a very holy woman. Pretending not to be quite sure what anniversary it was that we were celebrating, I said to her, "Sister, let me get this straight. Exactly how many years have you spent in the religious life?" Very humbly and first looking around to make sure there was no one else eavesdropping except God, she replied, "Honestly, Father, I've only spent one day in the religious life. Because every day I have to start all over again."

What a remarkable answer!

We human creatures bear within ourselves great riches and great weaknesses.

We are living temples, living churches. The Lord is within us, with the Holy Spirit. At catechism we're taught the seven gifts of the Holy Spirit. Obviously the Holy Spirit isn't so hard-up as to dispense only seven gifts. We only single out the main ones. But the Holy Spirit has remarkable gifts for each of us. There is no one on whom the Holy Spirit doesn't bestow a tailor-made, personalized minimum of charisms.

But to offset these riches there is always self-centeredness too. So we also single out the seven principal manifestations of self-centeredness, the "capital sins": envy, laziness, pride, impurity, avarice... But there are many more of them than that. They are called capital because each one of them gives rise to many other weaknesses.

God works this marvel: that even though he resides with us and in us, we still retain our weaknesses. It's up to us to avoid giving way to pride, to keep on the alert. We have to keep the process of conversion going all the time.   —*TTG*, 78

PRAYERS

We bless you Father, for the thirst you put in us, for the boldness you inspire, for the fire alight in us, that is you in us, you the just.

Never mind that our thirst is mostly unquenched (pity the satisfied). Never mind our bold plots are mostly unclinched, wanted not realized.

Who better than you knows that success comes not from us. You ask us to do our utmost only, but willingly.   —*DF,* 4

Hope without risk is not hope, which is believing in risky loving, trusting others in the dark, the blind leap, letting God take over.   —*DF,* 10

Father! Your Spirit told us through the mouth of Paul that the whole earth and we too as your children groan in the pains of a birth! It is easy, Lord, to grasp and affirm this. For there are passages too difficult and hours so filled with anguish that the image really applies: they are labor pains! Something is being born. Who knows? A world in which men and women can breathe, a more just, a more human world!
—*HAH,* 67

Ah, prayer! It's there every instant of your life! God is everywhere. Day and night we're plunged in the Lord. We walk, we talk, we live, we're always within the Lord. And God is within us. How beautiful it is to look at all of nature and to converse — not with words, but only by thought — with the Creator who is inside us!

That is incomparable strength — to know that we have the Holy Spirit. What wealth it is to discover the seven gifts the Spirit brings us all. We are so far from knowing how to use them well! What wealth it is to become aware of the particular gifts the Spirit has given to each of us, suited to each of us individually!

And what a privilege it is to believe that we are one with Christ! I like to say Cardinal Newman's beautiful prayer to Christ:

Lord Jesus, conceal Thyself not within me thus! Look Thou through my eyes, hear by my ears, speak by my mouth, walk with my feet! Lord, may my poor human presence recall, at least distantly, Thy divine presence! ...

With prayer and with the help of God's grace, our heart expands ever more and more toward the dimensions of the heart of Christ.

—*QL, 8, 10*

You know the prayer I love to say? "Lord, may your grace help me to want what you want, to prefer what you prefer ... For honestly, what do we know? We ought to do everything as though all depended on us, at the same putting ourselves into the Lord's hands, knowing that our own strength lies in offering him our weaknesses."   —*TTG, 58*

SOURCES

DF   *The Desert Is Fertile* (Maryknoll, NY: Orbis Books, 1974).

HAH   *Hoping against Hope* (Maryknoll, NY: Orbis Books, 1984).

QL   *Questions for Living* (Maryknoll, NY: Orbis Books, 1987).

TTG   *Through the Gospel with Dom Helder Camara* (Maryknoll, NY: Orbis Books, 1986).

THEA BOWMAN

A Gift to the Church

Thea Bowman was one of the great treasures of the American Catholic church. As a Franciscan Sister, she managed to integrate the resources of her Catholic faith with her identity as an African-American woman. Ablaze with the spirit of love, the memory of struggle, and a faith in God's promises, she impressed her many audiences not just with her message but with her nobility of spirit. No one she encountered, whether students, journalists, or a convention hall of bishops, could fail to catch a measure of her joy and gratitude for the gift of life. She was a particular inspiration to the black Catholic community, helping them to assert their pride of place among the People of God, while also encouraging them to enrich the wider church with the gifts of their distinctive culture and spirituality.

She was born Bertha Bowman in rural Mississippi in 1937. While attending a parochial school she was baptized as a Catholic at the age of ten. The most formative experience of her childhood came when her parents switched her to a new school run by the Franciscan Sisters of Perpetual Adoration. There she found her love of learning and also her vocation to become a nun. To her family and friends it was an astonishing decision. Nevertheless, she entered the convent when she was sixteen and took the name Sister Thea ("of God").

As the only black face in a white religious order she tended to stand out. But whatever the expectations of her community, she had no desire to "blend in." She brought with her a strong sense of her identity as a black Catholic woman, and over time she came to believe that this identity entailed a very special vocation. She was committed to asserting a black way of being Catholic. Previously black Catholics were expected to conform to the spirituality of the white Euro-American church. The gospel hymns, the spirituals, the dancing, the testifying in the spirit — all features of the Protestant black churches — were foreign in the Catholic church. But for black Catholics, Sister Thea believed, this accounted for a sense of cultural marginality. Not only should there be room in the Catholic church for the spiritual traditions of African Americans, but their experience had much to contribute to the wider church. Part of this experience was the history of slavery and oppression. But part of it also was a spirituality of survival and resistance reflected in the tradition of the spirituals, the importance of family, community, celebration, and remembrance.

"What does it mean to be black and Catholic?" she asked. "It means that I come to my church fully functioning. I bring myself, my black self, all that I am, all that I have, all that I hope to become. I bring my whole history, my traditions, my experience, my culture, my African-American song and dance and gesture and movement and teaching and preaching and healing and responsibility as gift to the Church."

After earning a doctorate in English, Thea returned to the South to work with the church in Mississippi and Louisiana. In 1980 she helped to found the Institute of Black Catholic Studies at Xavier University in New Orleans. This became the base for her ministry as a speaker and evangelist. Thea was an extraordinary, spellbinding speaker. A combination storyteller, preacher, and performer, she brought to her lectures the atmosphere of a revival meeting. Punctuating her speaking with renditions of the spirituals, she generally had her audiences, black or white, singing along with her before she was finished.

She was invited to speak before hundreds of groups, including the U.S. Catholic bishops at their annual meeting in 1989. In one speech she noted that women were not allowed to preach in the Catholic church. But this shouldn't stop them from preaching everywhere else! "God has called to us to speak the word that is Christ, that is truth, that is salvation. And if we speak that word in love and faith, with patience and prayer, and perseverance, it will take root. It does have power to save us. Call one another! Testify! Teach! Act on the Word! Witness!"

By this time Sister Thea was compelled to bear witness in a different way. She was diagnosed in 1984 as suffering from breast cancer. Though increasingly ill, Thea continued her extensive travels and speaking, even when she was confined to a wheelchair. With her bright African robes and her now-bald head, she was, as always, a striking figure. But now when she sang the spirituals — "Sometimes I feel like a motherless child /

A long way from home" — *her audience detected an even more personal and poignant confession of faith.*

The faith that had sustained the slaves, the hope expressed in the spirituals, the love embodied by St. Francis, now sustained her in her personal way of the cross. And to her other mighty gifts to the church she now added the witness of her courage and trust in God. Asked how she made sense out of her suffering, she answered, "I don't make sense of suffering. I try to make sense of life . . . I try each day to see God's will. I console myself with the old Negro spiritual, 'Soon I will be done the troubles of this world. I'm going home to live with God.' "

Sister Thea died on March 30, 1990, at the age of fifty-three.

SPIRITUALITY

Spirituality is conscious contact with the Spirit that is God, who is above us, who transcends and inspires us. It is a conscious contact with the spirit that is "self," with the inner-self where memory, imagination, intellect, feelings and the body are caught up in the search for humanity. Spirituality is conscious contact with the spirit that is community, with the chemistry, the dynamic that bonds us together when we are gathered in peak moments of joy or grief, struggle or aspiration. In a word, Spirituality is at once God-awareness, self-awareness, and other-awareness. It is the level of consciousnesses and of choosing that makes us different from the pelican that dies on the beach and simply is no more.

Spirituality is faith lived. As such it encompasses the totality of personal and collective responses to religious belief — relationships, morality, worship, and daily living. As Christians we strive to understand and to act in a way that makes us part of the reality that is the will and purpose of God. We strive to let ourselves feel, remember . . . that which we believe. Spirituality, then, is operative on cognitive, affective and volitional levels: It encompasses the whole person — their mind, heart, and will.

Black American Spirituality . . . is at once a response to and a reflection on Black life and culture. It is rooted in our African heritage, with its ways of perceiving and valuing reality, its style of expression, its modes of prayer and contemplating the divine. It is colored by our Middle Passage, Slavery, our Island and Latin experience, segregation, integration, and our on-going struggle for liberation . . .

While speaking of *a* Black Spirituality, it must be understood that Blacks are not all alike. The emphasis and expression of our Spirituality, therefore, is not all alike. There are uniquenesses within the collective. There are diverse preferences within our corporate spirituality. It is important to understand the collective reality, but this reality cannot be known in isolation from its constituent parts... In terms of Black Spirituality, the question becomes "How can we know, participate in, and impact the encounter with God, the mode and view of life of the Black people who make up my community?"

The answer to that question will only come if we can hear, see and be touched by the people. By constructing a framework for active listening, we can begin to grasp that magnitude of the oral and aural tradition which is the most eloquent expression of Black Spirituality.

— *Shooting Star*, 38–40

BEING A BLACK CATHOLIC

From Thea Bowman's address to the U.S. bishops on June 17, 1989. She began by singing "Sometimes I feel like a motherless child / A long way from home," and asked: "Can you hear me church, will you help me church? I'm a pilgrim in the journey looking for home, and Jesus told me the church is my home, and Jesus told me that heaven is my home and I have here no lasting city. Cardinals, archbishops, bishops: My brothers or church, please help me to get home."

What does it mean to be black and Catholic? It means that I come to my church fully functioning. That doesn't frighten you, does it? I come to my church fully functioning. I bring myself, my black self, all that I am, all that I have, all that I hope to become, I bring my whole history, my tradition, my experience, my culture, my African-American song and dance and gesture and movement and teaching and preaching and healing and responsibility as gift to the church.

I bring a ... spirituality [that] is contemplative and biblical and holistic, bringing to religion a totality of minds and imagination, of memory, of feeling and passion and emotion and intensity, of faith that is embodied, incarnate praise ... a spirituality that is communal, that tries to walk and talk and work and pray and play together — even with the bishops. You know, when our bishop is around, we want him to be where we can find him, where we can reach out and touch him, where we can talk to him. Don't be too busy, you-all.

A spirituality that in the middle of your Mass or in the middle of your sermon just might have to shout out and say, "Amen, hallelujah, thank you Jesus." A faith that attempts to be Spirit-filled. The old ladies say that if you love the Lord your God with your whole heart, [with] your whole soul and your whole mind and all your strength, then you praise the Lord with your whole heart and soul and mind and strength and you don't bring him any feeble service.

If you get enough fully functioning black Catholics in your diocese, they are going to hold up the priest and they are going to hold up the bishops. We love our bishops, you-all. We love you-all too. But see, these bishops are our own, ordained for the church universal, ordained for the service of God's people, but they are ours; we raised them; they came from our community and in a unique way they can speak for us and to us. And that's what the church is talking about. Indigenous leadership. The leaders are supposed to look like the folks, ain't that what the church says?

To be black and Catholic means to realize that the work of the ordained ministers is not a threat to me and I'm no threat to that. The work of the ordained minister, of the professional minister, is to enable the people of God to do the work of the church. To feed us sacramentally, to enable us to preach and to teach, and I ain't necessarily talking about preaching in the pulpit.

You know as well as I do that some of the best preaching does not go on in the pulpit, for as a Catholic Christian I have a responsibility to preach and to teach, to worship and to pray. Black folk can't just come into church and depend on the preacher and say, "Let Father do it." And if Father doesn't do it right, then they walk out and they complain, you know, "That liturgy didn't do anything for me."

The question that we raise is, What did you do for the liturgy? And the church is calling us to be participatory and to be involved. The church is calling us to feed and to clothe and to shelter and to teach. Your job is to enable me, to enable God's people, black people, white people, brown people, all the people, to do the work of the church in the modern world. Teaching, preaching, witnessing, worshipping, serving, healing and reconciling in black, because wedded to the lived experience, to the history and the heritage of black people.

Getting in touch. To be black and Catholic means to get in touch with the world church, with my brothers and sisters in Rome, with my brothers and sisters in China, with my brothers and sisters in Europe and Asia and Latin America, with the church of Africa. Do your folk realize that there are more Catholic Christians in Africa than in North America? . . .

Black people are still victims within the church of paternalism, of a patronizing attitude, black people who within the church have developed a mission mentality — they don't feel called, they don't feel responsible, they don't do anything. Let Father do it, let the Sisters do it, let the friends and benefactors from outside do it. That's the mission mentality, and it kills us and it kills our churches. And so, within the church, how can we work together so that all of us have equal access to input, equal access to opportunity, equal access to participation?

Go into a room and look around and see who's missing and send some of our folks out to call them in so that the church can be what she claims to be, truly Catholic.

They still talk about black folk in the church. You hear it, you know, you hear it over the sidelines. They say we're lazy. They say we're loud. They say we're irresponsible. They say we lower the standards. So often we've been denied the opportunities to learn and to practice. You learned by trial and error; ain't that how you learned?

Some black people don't approve of black religious expression in Catholic liturgy. They have been told that it's not properly Catholic. They've been told that it's not appropriately serious or dignified or solemn or controlled, that the European way is necessarily the better way.

How can we teach all the people what it means to be black and Catholic? The *National Catechetical Directory* says that all catechesis is supposed to be multicultural, but how little of it is. When we attempt to bring our black gifts to the church, people who do not know us say we're being non-Catholic or separatists or just plain uncouth...

We have come a long way in faith. Just look where we have come from. We as black people find ourselves at the threshold of a new age. And as I look about the room I know that many of you have walked and talked and worked and prayed and stood with us in a society and in the church. And in the name of all black folk, I thank you.

Today we're called to walk together in a new way toward that land of promise and to celebrate who we are and whose we are. If we as church walk together, don't let nobody separate you. That's one thing black folk can teach you. Don't let folk divide you or put the lay folk over here and the clergy over there, put the bishops in one room and the clergy in the other room, put the women over here and the men over there.

The church teaches us that the church is a family. It is a family of families and the family got to stay together. We know that if we do stay together, if we walk and talk and work and play and stand together in

Jesus' name, we'll be who we say we are, truly Catholic; and we shall overcome — overcome the poverty, overcome the loneliness, overcome the alienation and build together a holy city, a new Jerusalem, a city set apart where they'll know we are his because we love one another.

> [*Singing*]
> We shall overcome
> We shall overcome
> We shall overcome someday.
> Oh, deep in my heart,
> Deep in my heart I know,
> I do believe,
> we shall overcome someday.

Now, bishops, I'm going to ask you-all to do something. Cross your right over your left hand. You've got to move together to do that. All right now, walk with me. See, in the old days, you had to tighten up so that when the bullets would come, so that when the tear gas would come, so that when the dogs would come, so that when the horses would come, so that when the tanks would come brothers and sisters would not be separated from one another.

And you remember what they did with the clergy and the bishops in those old days, where they'd put them? Right up in front, to lead the people in solidarity with our brothers and sisters in the church who suffer in South Africa, who suffer in Poland, who suffer in Ireland, who suffer in Nicaragua, in Guatemala, in Northern Ireland, all over this world. We shall live in love.

> [*Singing*]
> We shall live in love
> We shall live in love
> We shall live in love today.
> Oh, deep in my heart,
> Deep in my heart I know,
> I do believe,
> We shall live in love today.

That's all we've got to do: love the Lord, to love our neighbor. Amen. Amen. Amen. Amen. — *Shooting Star*, 32–37

WOMEN IN THE CHURCH

When I was a little girl in Canton, Mississippi, I went to those old black churches and I learned what they called the old-time religion. I wanted to grow up so I could be a preacher.

Now you know women can't preach in the Catholic church. But that's not bothering me this morning. I can't preach in the church. Women can't preach in the Catholic church. But I can preach in the streets. I can preach in the neighborhood. I can preach in the home. I can preach and teach in the family. And it's the preaching that's done in the home that brings life and meaning to the Word your priest proclaims in his official ministry in the pulpit...

I invite all of you to pause a moment and bring to mind the women who gave you life, who nurtured you, who gave you light and laughter and faith and love. Did those women preach, did they teach, did they testify, did they witness?

Charles de Foucauld once said that every Christian is called to shout the Good News of the Lord Jesus Christ from the rooftops, not in words, but in life. We're all called to preach, to shout the Good News by our lives. Never too young, never too old to share life, faith, and love. A few years ago you hardly ever heard of people getting senile in the black community. [They were] too busy preaching, too busy teaching, too busy testifying and witnessing, too busy sharing life, death, and love. An old song says, "Keep so busy serving my Master and God fur to die."

Sharing life and faith and love are all our business, but in a special way and by a special calling — giving life, sustaining life, sharing life have always been life for women. Married or single, young or old, rich or poor, in sickness and in health, in life and in death, so long as we have breath and being, we are called to be life-givers and life-nourishers and life-sustainers.

In the scriptural reading for today from the Book of Deuteronomy, we heard Moses tell the people to hear the statutes, observe the teachings, keep the commandments, and they will be wise and intelligent, and God will be close to them. Isn't that what your Mama told you? Or your grandmother, aunt, or whoever mothered you in the Spirit?...

The Word of God became Incarnate. We are called to preach that word day by day by day — in our homes, in our families, in our neighborhood — to bear witness, to testify, to shout it from the rooftops with our lives. Ladies, we are called to plant that Word in the minds and hearts and souls of our children, husbands, lovers, fathers, brothers, uncles, nephews, and friends. We don't have to worry about deception and hypocrisy... They know when our witness is the fruit of our effort and struggle and sincerity.

God has called to us to speak the word that is Christ, that is truth, that is salvation. And if we speak that word in love and faith, with patience and prayer and perseverance, it will take root. It does have power to save us. Call one another! Testify! Teach! Act on the Word! Witness!

—*Shooting Star,* 76–78

LET ME LIVE UNTIL I DIE

These excerpts from interviews with Thea Bowman, conducted in the year before she died, appeared in Praying *magazine and* US Catholic.

What kind of changes have you had to make in your life because of the cancer?

Part of my approach to my illness has been to say I want to choose life, I want to keep going, I want to live fully until I die...

I don't know what my future holds. In the meantime, I am making a conscious effort to learn to live with discomfort, and, at the same time, to go about my work. I find that when I am involved in the business of life, when I'm working with people, particularly with children, I feel better. A kind of strength and energy comes with that.

How do you find yourself talking with God about your illness? Has it changed your prayer?

I was reared in a community in which prayer was natural... consistent, [and] shared. Something good would happen and some old woman would just break out in prayer. Very early, I learned traditional black modalities of prayer — words, symbols, phrases, songs, prayers.

Older folks used to say God is my father and my mother and my sister and brother, my pearl of great price, my lily of the valley, my rock, my sword, my shield, God's a god of peace. God's a god of war. God's water when you're thirsty, bread when you're hungry. God is my doctor, my lawyer, my captain in the battle of life, my friend, my king.

I find that the old prayers come back to me. For example, I recall an old man who would get up in church and say, "I thank you for another day of life because this very night many folks have been laid out on their cooling boards. I ask you for strength to bear the burdens of the day. I know that whatever comes to me is sanctioned by your holy hand." The old styles of prayer bring me comfort.

Had you gotten out of the habit of these old prayers?

Not really, but when I'm tired, weak and in pain, I find myself turning to these prayers quicker than I used to. When I hurt I like to sing some of the old songs: "Precious Lord, take my hand, lead me on, let me stand. I'm tired, I'm weak and I'm worn. Through the storm, through the night, lead me on to the light. Take my hand, Precious Lord, lead me on." I find that prayer and song can take me beyond the pain.

Our old folk would go to church and pray and they'd come home happy. Within the traditional prayer of the black community, there were ways of controlling the mind, the mood and even the body, and doing it in Jesus' name. I thank God for that gift of my people...

Our prayer tradition attempts to go to God with feeling and passion and emotion and intensity. I want to be a part of what Jesus felt as he hung on the cross. I want to feel the anguish. I want to feel the love that motivated him to save us. He's the Almighty Word who leapt down from heaven. He's the son of the eternal father who became human like us in all things save sin. Yet, he accepted the sufferings of a lifetime as a human being to give us life. I want to feel that love, that compassion...

Speaking of "keeping on," what's ahead for you now?

Live for a while and then death. It's as simple as that. When I first found out I had cancer, I didn't know what to pray for. I didn't know if I should pray for healing or life or death. Then I found peace in praying for what my folks call "God's perfect will." As it evolved, my prayer has become, "Lord, let me live until I die." By that I mean I want to live, love, and serve fully until death comes. If that prayer is answered, if I am able to live until I die, how long really doesn't matter. Whether it's just a few months or a few years is really immaterial.

I grew up with people who believed you could serve the Lord from a sickbed or a deathbed. The great commandment is to love the Lord your God with your whole heart, your whole soul, your whole mind, and all your strength. As long as I have my mental facility, I want to keep on loving. I want to keep on serving. That's what I hope to be about.

My illness has helped me to realize how fragile our hold on life is. I always thought I was going to live to be an old woman, like my mother and my father and all the other old people I know and was close to when I was a child. But I no longer think that. My time isn't long. Now I just want to find ways to make the most of the time I have left...

◆ ◆ ◆

How do you make sense out of your pain and suffering?

I don't make sense of it. I try to make sense of life. I try to keep myself open to people and to laughter and to love and to have faith. I try each day to see God's will. I pray, "Oh Jesus, I surrender." I pray, "Father, take this cross away. Not my will, but thy will be done." I console myself with the old Negro spiritual: "Soon I will be done the troubles of this world. I'm going home to live with God."

Is God really present in suffering?

God is present in everything. In the universe, in creation, in me and all that happens to me, in my brothers and sisters, in the church, and in the Eucharist — everywhere. In the midst of suffering. I feel God's presence and cry out to God for help: "Lord, help me to hold on."

Why do people have to suffer? What possible good can come from it?

I don't know. Why is there war? Why is there hunger? Why is there pain? Perhaps it's an incentive for struggling human beings to reach out to one another, to help one another, to love one another, to be blessed and strengthened and humanized in the process. Perhaps it's an incentive to see Christ in our world and to view the work of Christ and to feel the suffering of Christ.

I know that suffering gives us new perspective and helps us to clarify our real value. I know that suffering has helped me to clarify my relationships... Perhaps suffering stops us in our tracks and forces us to confront what is real within ourselves and in our environment...

Has your faith changed since you discovered you had cancer?

My faith is simpler. In many ways, it's easier; it's closer to home and to reality. I have more desire to grow in faith and hope and love. When I'm in pain, I know I need Jesus to walk with me. I can't make it on my own. I pray, "Lord, I believe. Increase my faith. Help my unbelief."

I remember the words of an old song: "We've come this far by faith, leaning on the Lord, trusting in his words. The Lord has never failed us yet. Oh, can't turn around because we've come this way by faith." ...

Has your image of God changed?

My people graced me with multiple images of the living God.

God is bread when you're hungry, water when you're thirsty, a harbor from the storm. God's a father to the fatherless, a mother to the motherless. God's my sister, my brother, my leader, my guide, my teacher, my comforter, my friend. God's the way-maker and burden-bearer, a heart-fixer and a mind-regulator. God's my doctor who never lost a patient, my lawyer who never lost a case, my captain who never lost a battle. God's my all in all, my everything.

God's my rock, my sword, my shield, my lily of the valley, my pearl of great price. God's a god of peace and a god of war. Counselor, Emmanuel, Redeemer, Savior, Prince of Peace, Son of God, Mary's little baby, wonderful Word of God.

These images come from Scripture and from the meditations of Christians ... I meditate on each one of these images on a particular day at a particular time. Each one corresponds to a particular need. All these images help me as I call upon God's name ...

Do you find hope in yourself?

I know that God is using me in ways beyond my comprehension. God has given me the grace to see some of the seeds that I have sown bear good fruit, and I am so grateful.

Do you ever despair?

What for? I don't despair because I believe God leads me and guides me, and I believe that I can reach out for God's hand. I have received such love and so many gifts. That's a part of what I hope at this time in my life to be able to share. I want to say to people just keep on keeping on.

— *Shooting Star,* 125–31

SOURCE

Sister Thea Bowman, *Shooting Star: Selected Speeches and Writings,* ed. Celestine Cepress, FSPA (Winona, MN: Saint Mary's Press, 1993).

ELEVEN

HENRI NOUWEN

A Wounded Healer

🔲🔲🔲🔲🔲🔲🔲🔲

At the time of his death in 1996, Henri Nouwen was one of the most popular and influential spiritual writers of his time. Through dozens of books he invited countless persons to enter more deeply into the spiritual life — intimacy with Jesus and solidarity with a wounded world. Much of his impact came from his frank willingness to confide his own woundedness. This confessional honesty was a central feature of his message. The spiritual life, he insisted, was not simply intended for saints or "perfect people." Instead, the call of Jesus was addressed to the lame and halt, ordinary people, everyone in their brokenness and humanity: "We have been chosen to make our own limited and very conditional love the gateway for the unlimited and unconditional love of God." It was a call to conversion, to healing, a call to come home.

The search for his true home was a constant motif of Nouwen's life and writings. Born in Holland where he was ordained a priest, Nouwen spent the better part of his life in North America. He taught at a number of prestigious American universities, including Notre Dame and Yale Divinity School. During the 1970s he began to emerge as a popular author through such titles as The Wounded Healer *and* Intimacy. *Though he acquired a devoted following, he experienced a constant restlessness and anxiety about his place in the world. He was afflicted by an inordinate need for affection and affirmation; it seemed there was a depth within that God alone could fill.*

In 1974 Nouwen took a year off to live in the Trappist Abbey of the Genesee. It was not enough to teach spirituality; he felt he must cultivate some deeper spiritual center of his own. His subsequent Genesee Diary *offered a moving account of this monastic retreat, while at the same time opening a window on his spiritual struggles. "What was driving me from one book to another, one place to another, one project to another?" In 1981 he went to Latin America, wondering whether God was calling him to some kind of ministry in the barrios of Bolivia or Peru. Instead, in 1982, he accepted an invitation to teach at Harvard Divinity School. His lectures there attracted enormous crowds. But his popularity only underlined his sense of loneliness and isolation. Later he wrote with feeling about the temptations that Christ suffered in the desert: to be "relevant, powerful, and spectacular."*

At this point there came a great turning point in his life. Over the years Nouwen had visited a number of L'Arche communities in France and Canada. In these communities disabled people live together with able helpers. In 1986 he received a formal invitation from Daybreak, the L'Arche community in Toronto, to become their chaplain. It was the first time in his life he had received such a formal call. With trepidation he accepted, and Daybreak became his home for the last ten years of his life.

It was unlike anything he had ever known. Nouwen had written extensively about community, but he had never really known community life. A man of great intellectual gifts, he was physically clumsy and was challenged by such everyday tasks as parking a car or making a sandwich.

Like other members of L'Arche, Nouwen was assigned the care of one of the residents, a young man named Adam — in fact, one of the most severely handicapped adults in the community. Nouwen spent hours each morning simply bathing, dressing, and feeding Adam. Some of his old admirers wondered whether Henri Nouwen was not wasting his talents in such menial duties. But to his surprise he found this an occasion for deep inner conversion. Adam was not impressed by Nouwen's books or his fame or his genius as a public speaker. But through this mute and helpless man, Nouwen began to know what it meant to be "beloved" of God.

This was not, however, the end of his struggles. After his first year at Daybreak Nouwen suffered a nervous breakdown — the culmination of long suppressed tensions. For months he could barely talk or leave his room. Now he was the helpless one, mutely crying out for some affirmation of his existence. As he later described it, "Everything came crashing down — my self-esteem, my energy to live and work, my sense of being loved, my hope for healing, my trust in God . . . everything." It was an experience of total darkness, a "bottomless abyss." During these months of anguish, he often wondered if God was real or just a product of his imagination.

But later he wrote, "I now know that while I felt completely abandoned, God didn't leave me alone." With the support of his friends and intensive counseling he was able to break through and to emerge more whole, more at peace with himself. Above all he emerged with a deeper trust in what he called "the inner voice of love," a voice calling him "beyond the boundaries of my short life, to where Christ is all in all."

In the summer of 1996 Nouwen was working hard, struggling to complete five books. To many friends he seemed happier and more relaxed than they had ever seen him. Thus it came as a great shock when he suddenly died of a heart attack on September 21 while passing through Amsterdam on his way to work on a documentary about his favorite painting, Rembrandt's "Return of the Prodigal Son."

He left many books in production, including a memoir of Adam, who had died that year. One of these books, published in the week of Nouwen's death, concluded with these words: "Many friends and family members have died during the past eight years and my own death is not so far away. But I have heard the inner voice of love, deeper and stronger than ever. I want to keep trusting in that voice, and be led by it beyond the boundaries of my short life, to where Christ is all in all."

DOWNWARD MOBILITY

We will never come to know our true vocation in life unless we are willing to grapple with the radical claim the gospel places on us. During the past twenty centuries many Christians have heard this radical call and have responded to it in true obedience...

Regardless of the particular shape we give to our lives, Jesus' call to discipleship is primal, all-encompassing, all-inclusive, demanding a total commitment. One cannot be a little bit for Christ, give him some attention, or make him one of many concerns.

Is it possible to follow Christ while fulfilling the demands of the world, to listen to Christ while paying equal attention to others, to carry Christ's cross while carrying many other burdens as well? Jesus certainly appears to draw a very sharp distinction. "No one can be the slave of two masters" (Matt. 6:24)...

These challenging words are not meant only for a few of Jesus' followers who have a so-called "special vocation." Rather, they are for all those who consider themselves Christians. They indicate the radical nature of the call. There is no easy way to follow Christ...

Our lives in this technological and highly competitive society are characterized by a pervasive drive for upward mobility. It is difficult for us even to imagine ourselves outside of this upwardly mobile lifestyle. Our whole way of living is structured around climbing the ladder of success and making it to the top...

The problem is not in the desire for development and progress as an individual or a community, but in making upward mobility itself into a religion. In this religion we believe that success means God is with us while failure means that we have sinned. The question then is, "Is God running with us?" If so, then God will make us win...

The story of our salvation stands radically over and against the philosophy of upward mobility. The great paradox which Scripture reveals to us is that real and total freedom is only found through downward mobility. The Word of God came down to us and lived among us as a slave. The divine way is indeed the downward way.

In the center of our faith as Christians stands the mystery that God chose to reveal the divine mystery by unreserved submission to the downward pull. God not only chose an insignificant people to carry the Word of salvation through the centuries, not only chose a small remnant of those people to fulfill God's promises, not only chose a humble girl in an unknown town in Galilee to become the temple of the Word, but God also chose to manifest the fullness of divine love in a man whose life led to a humiliating death outside the walls of the city...

Jesus leaves little doubt that the way he lived is the way he offers to his followers... With great persistence he points out the downward way: "Anyone who wants to be great among you must be your servant, just as the Son of Man came not to be served but to serve" (Matt 20: 26–28). The downward way is the way of the cross: "Anyone who does not take his cross and follow in my footsteps is not worthy of me. Anyone who finds his life will lose it; anyone who loses his life for my sake will find it" (Matt 10:39).

The disciple is the one who follows Jesus on his downward path and thus enters with him into new life. The gospel radically subverts the presuppositions of our upwardly mobile society. It is a jarring and unsettling challenge.

Yet, when we have carefully looked into the eyes of the poor, the oppressed, and the lowly, when we have paid humble attention to their ways of living, and when we have listened gently to their observations and perceptions, we might have already a glimpse of the truth Jesus spoke about...

Somewhere deep in our hearts we already know that success, fame, influence, power, and money do not give us the inner joy and peace we crave. Somewhere we can even sense a certain envy of those who have shed all false ambitions and found a deeper fulfillment in their relationship with God. Yes, somewhere we can even get a taste of that mysterious joy in the smile of those who have nothing to lose.

Then we begin to perceive that the downward road is not the road to hell, but the road to heaven. Keeping this in mind can help us accept the fact that in the Reign of God the poor are the messengers of the good news...

The downward way is God's way, not ours. God is revealed as God to us in the downward pull, because only the One who is God can be emptied of divine privilege and become as we are. The great mystery upon which our faith rests is that the One who is in no way like us, who cannot be compared with us, nor enter into competition with us, has come among us and taken on our mortal flesh...

Downward mobility is the divine way, the way of the cross, the way of Christ. It is precisely this divine way of living that our Lord wants to give to us through his Spirit...

The way of the cross, the downward mobility of God, becomes our way not because we try to imitate Jesus, but because we are transformed into living Christs by our relationship with his Spirit. The spiritual life is the life of the Spirit of Christ in us, a life that sets us free to be strong while weak, to be free while captive, to be joyful while in pain, to be rich while poor, to be on the downward way of salvation while living in the midst of an upwardly mobile society.

Although this spiritual life may well seem enigmatic, intangible, and elusive to us who live in a scientific age, its fruits leave little doubt about the radical transformation it brings about. Love, joy, peace, patience, kindness, goodness, trustfulness, gentleness, and self-control are indeed the qualities of our Lord himself and reveal his presence in the midst of a world so torn apart by idolatry, envy, greed, sexual irresponsibility, war, and other sin... It is not hard to distinguish the upward pull of our world from the downward pull of Christ...

We will never be without struggle. But when we persevere with hope, courage, and confidence, we will come to fully realize in our innermost being that through the downward road of Christ we will enter with him into his glory. So let us be grateful for our vocation, resist our temptation, and be ever committed to a life of ongoing formation.

— *The Selfless Way of Christ*

THE EUCHARISTIC LIFE

The following selections are taken from With Burning Hearts, *in which Nouwen uses the story of the disciples on the road to Emmaus as the foundation for his reflections on the "Eucharistic life." In the midst of their sorrow, the disciples encounter a mysterious stranger on the road. He explains to them the meaning of the Word. They invite him to stay with them and they recognize him finally in the "breaking of the bread." Inspired, they go out to report what they have seen and witnessed.*

"Lord, Have Mercy"

I often wonder how I would live if there were not resentment at all in my heart. I am so used to talking about people I do not like, to harboring memories about events that gave me much pain, or to acting with suspicion and fear that I do not know how it would be if there were nothing to complain about and nobody to gripe about! My heart still has many corners that hide my resentments and I wonder if I really want to be without them. What would I do without these resentments? . . .

I wonder if there are any people without resentments. Resentment is such an obvious response to our many losses. The tragedy is that much resentment is hidden within the church. It is one of the most paralyzing aspects of the Christian community.

Still, the Eucharist presents another option. It is the possibility to choose, not resentment, but gratitude. Mourning our losses is the first step away from resentment and toward gratitude. The tears of our grief can soften our hardened hearts and open us to the possibility to say "thanks."

The word "Eucharist" means literally "act of thanksgiving. To celebrate the Eucharist and to live a Eucharistic life has everything to do with Gratitude. Living Eucharistically is living life as a gift, a gift for which one is grateful . . .

Each Eucharist begins with a cry for God's mercy...This cry for mercy is possible when we are willing to confess that somehow, somewhere, we ourselves have something to do with our losses. Crying for mercy is a recognition that blaming God, the world, or others for our losses does not do full justice to the truth of who we are...Celebrating the Eucharist requires that we stand in this world accepting our co-responsibility for the evil that surrounds and pervades us...

"Lord, have mercy, Lord, have mercy, Lord, have mercy." That's the prayer that keeps emerging from the depth of our being and breaking through the walls of our cynicism. Yes, we are sinners...Still, there is a voice: "My grace is enough for you!" and we cry again for the healing of our cynical hears and dare to believe that, indeed, in the midst of our mourning, we can find a gift to be grateful for. For this discovery we need a special companion!

"This Is the Word of God"

Jesus joins us as we walk in sadness and explains the scriptures to us. But we do not know that it is Jesus. We think of him as a stranger who knows less than we do of what is happening in our lives. And still — we know something, we sense something, we intuit something: our hearts begin to burn...

It is with this mysterious presence that the "service of the Word" during each Eucharist wants to bring us in touch, and it is this same mysterious presence that is constantly revealed to us as we live our lives Eucharistically...

It is important to know that, although these words, read or spoken, are there to inform, instruct, or inspire us, their first significance is that they make Jesus himself present to us...Without that presence through the word, we won't be able to recognize his presence in the breaking of the bread...

We need the word spoken and explained by the one who joins us on the road and makes his presence known to us — a presence first discerned in our burning hearts. It is this presence that encourages us to let go of our hardened hearts and become grateful. As grateful people we can invite into the intimacy of our home the one who has made our hearts burn.

"I Believe"

Maybe we are not used to thinking about the Eucharist as an invitation to Jesus to stay with us. We are more inclined to think about Jesus inviting us to his house, his table, his meal, but Jesus wants to be invited. Without an invitation he will go on to other places...Unless we invite him, he will always remain a stranger...with whom we had an interesting conversation, but a stranger nevertheless...

Jesus reveals himself to us as the Good Shepherd who knows us intimately and loves us. But do we want to be known by him? Do we want him to walk freely into every room of our inner lives?...

When, after the readings and the homily, we say: "I believe in God, Father, Son, and Holy Spirit, in the Catholic Church, the communion of saints, the forgiveness of sins, the resurrection of the body, and life everlasting," we invite Jesus into our home and entrust ourselves to his Way.

"Take and Eat"

When Jesus enters into the home of his disciples, it becomes his home. The guest becomes host. He who was invited now invites...

"Now while he was with them at table, he took the bread and said the blessing; then he broke it and handed it to them." So simple, so ordinary, so obvious, and still — so very different! What else can you do when you share bread with your friends? You take it, bless it, break it, and give it. That is what bread is for: to be taken, blessed, broken, and given. Nothing new, nothing surprising. It happens every day, in countless homes. It belongs to the essence of living. We can't really live without bread that is taken, blessed, broken and given. Without it there is no table fellowship, no community, no bond of friendship, no peace, no love, no hope. Yet, with it, all can become new!...

Every time we invite Jesus into our homes, that is to say, into our life with all its light and dark sides, and offer him the place of honor at our table, he takes the bread and the cup and hands them to us saying, "Take and eat, this is my body. Take and drink, this is my blood. Do this to remember me." Are we surprised? Not really! Wasn't our heart burning when he talked to us on the road? Didn't we already know that he was not a stranger to us?...

The Eucharist is the most ordinary and the most divine gesture imaginable. That is the truth of Jesus. So human, yet so divine; so familiar, yet so mysterious; so close, yet so revealing!...

Jesus is God-for-us, God-with-us, God-within-us. Jesus is God giving himself completely, pouring himself out for us without reserve. Jesus doesn't hold back or cling to his own possessions. He gives all there is to give. "Eat, drink, this is my body, this is my blood...this is me for you!"...

The word that best expresses this mystery of God's total self-giving love is "communion." It is the word that contains the truth that, in and through Jesus, God wants not only to teach us, instruct us, or inspire us, but to become one with us...

It is this intense desire of God to enter into the most intimate relationship with us that forms the core of the Eucharistic celebration and the Eucharistic life. God not only wants to enter human history...but God wants to become our daily food and drink at any time and any place...

Eucharist is recognition. It is the full realization that the one who takes, blesses, breaks, and gives is the One who, from the beginning of time, has desired to enter into communion with us.

"Go and Tell"

The Eucharist concludes with a mission. "Go now and tell!" The Latin words "Ite Missa est," with which the priest used to conclude the Mass, literally means: "Go, this is your mission."

Communion is not the end. Mission is. Communion, that sacred intimacy with God, is not the final moment of the Eucharistic life. We recognized him, but that recognition is not just for us to savor or to keep as a secret. As Mary of Magdala, so too the two friends [on the road to Emmaus] had heard deep in themselves the words, "Go and tell." That's the conclusion of the Eucharistic celebration; that too is the final call of the Eucharistic life. "Go and tell. What you have heard and seen is not just for yourself. It is for the brothers and sisters and for all who are ready to receive it."...

It is not just the Eucharist, but the *Eucharistic life* that makes the difference. Each day, yes, each moment of the day, there is the pain of our losses and the opportunity to listen to a word that asks us to choose to live these losses as a way to glory. Each day, too, there is the possibility to invite the stranger into our home and to let him break the bread for us. The Eucharistic celebration has summarized for us what our life of faith is all about, and we have to go home to live it as long and as fully as we can...

In the Eucharist we are asked to leave the table and go to our friends to discover with them that Jesus is truly alive and calls us together to become a new people — a people of the resurrection...

The Eucharist is always mission. The Eucharist that has freed us from our paralyzing sense of loss and revealed to us that the Spirit of Jesus lives within us empowers us to go out into the world and to bring good news to the poor, sight to the blind, liberty to the captives, and to proclaim that God has shown again his favor to all people. But we are not sent out alone; we are sent with our brothers and sisters who also know that Jesus lives within them.

The movement flowing from the Eucharist is the movement from communion to community to ministry. Our experience of communion first sends us to our brothers and sisters to share with them our stories and build with them a body of love. Then, as community, we can move in all directions and reach out to all people...

It belongs to the essence of the Eucharistic life to make this circle of love grow. Having entered into communion with Jesus and created community with those who know that he is alive, we now can go and join the many lonely travelers and help them discover that they too have the gift of love to share... Every time there is a real encounter leading from despair to hope and from bitterness to gratitude, we will see some of the darkness being dispelled and life, once again, breaking through the boundaries of death.

This has been, and continues to be, the experience of those who live a Eucharistic life.   — *With Burning Hearts*

PRAYER AND PEACEMAKING

On August 6, 1945, the day on which the atom bomb was first used in war, peacemaking came to mean what it could not have meant before; the task of saving humanity from collective suicide... On that day the blessing on peacemakers became the blessing for our century... There are many other urgent tasks to accomplish: the work of worship, evangelization, healing of church divisions, alleviating worldwide poverty and hunger, and defending human rights. But all of these tasks are closely connected with the task that stands above them all: making peace...

Peacemaking can no longer be regarded as peripheral to being a Christian. It is not something like joining the parish choir. Nobody can be a Christian without being a peacemaker. The issue is not that we have

the occasional obligation to give some of our attention to war preven-
tion, or even that we should be willing to give some of our free time
to activities in the service of peace. What we are called to is a *life* of
peacemaking in which all that we do, say, think, or dream is part of our
concern to bring peace to this world. Just as Jesus' command to love one
another cannot be seen as a part-time obligation, but requires a total
investment and dedication, so too Jesus' call to peacemaking is unconditional, unlimited, and uncompromising. None of us is excused!...The
tragedy is that, in some demonic way, the word "peace" has become
tainted. For many people this most precious word has become associated with sentimentalism, utopianism, radicalism, romanticism, and
even with irresponsibility...

Christians today, if they want to be Christians, have to find the
courage to make the word "peace" as important as the word "freedom."
There should be no doubt in the minds of the people who inhabit this
world that Christians are peacemakers.

A peacemaker prays. Prayer is the beginning and the end, the source
and the fruit, the core and the content, the basis and the goal of all
peacemaking. I say this without apology, because it allows me to go
straight to the heart of the matter, which is that peace is a divine gift, a
gift we receive in prayer.

In his farewell discourse Jesus said to his apostles, "Peace I leave to
you, my own peace I give to you; a peace the world cannot give, this is
my gift to you" (John 14:27). When we want to make peace we first of
all have to move away from the dwelling places of those who hate peace
and enter into the house of him who offers us his peace. This entering
into a new dwelling place is what prayer is all about.

The invitation to a life of prayer is the invitation to live in the midst
of this world without being dropped in the net of its wounds and needs.
The word "Prayer" stands for a radical interruption of the vicious chain
of interlocking dependencies that lead to violence and war and for an
entering into an entirely new dwelling place. It points to a new way of
speaking, of breathing, of being together, of knowing — truly, to a whole
new way of living.

It is not easy to express the radical change that prayer represents, since
for many the word "prayer" is associated with piety: talking to God,
thinking about God, attending morning and evening worship, going to
Sunday service, saying grace before meals, and many other things. All of

these have something to do with prayer, but when I speak about prayer as the basis for peacemaking I speak first of all about moving away from the dwelling place of those who hate peace into the house of God. Prayer is the center of Christian life. It is the only necessary thing (Luke 10:42). It is living with God, here and now...

On the evening before his death he says to his friends, "Make your home in me, as I make mine in you... Whoever remains in me, with me in him, bears fruit in plenty" (John 15:4–5). This divine dwelling place enables us to live as peacemakers in a hostile world like sheep among wolves... Prayer is the new language that belongs to the new house...

Prayer means entering into communion with the One who loved us before we could love. It is this "first love" (1 John 4:19) that is revealed to us in prayer. The deeper we enter into the house of God, the house whose language is prayer, the less dependent we are on the blame or praise of those who surround us, and the freer we are to let our whole being be filled with that first love...

In prayer, however, again and again, we discover that the love we are looking for has already been given to us and that we can come to the experience of that love. Prayer is entering into communion with the One who molded our being in our mother's womb with love and only love. There, in that first love, lies our true self, a self not made up of the rejections and acceptances of those with whom we live, but solidly rooted in the One who called us into existence. In the house of God we were created. To that house we are called to return. Prayer is the act of returning.

Prayer is the basis of all peacemaking precisely because in prayer we come to the realization that we do not belong to the world in which conflicts and wars take place, but to him who offers us his peace. The paradox of peacemaking is indeed that we can speak of peace in this world only when our sense of who we are is not anchored in the world. We can say, "We are for peace," only when those who are fighting have no power over us. We can bear witness for the Prince of Peace only when our trust is in him and him alone. In short, we can be in this world only when we no longer belong to it. This moving out of the world of warmakers in order to be in it as peacemakers is the Way of the Cross, which Jesus shows us. It is the long process of conversion in which we die to our old identity that is rooted in the ups and downs of worldly praise for all we do in the service of peace. Only by living in the house of peace can we come to know what peacemaking will mean.

This might sound very remote from the concrete down-to-earth daily problems we have to deal with. But the opposite is true. Only by opening ourselves to the language and way of prayer can we cope with the interruptions, demands, and ordinary tasks of life without becoming fragmented and resentful. Prayer — living in the presence of God — is the most radical peace action we can imagine.

If we can come to the realization that it is in and through prayer that we find our true self, we already have a glimpse of its peacemaking quality. When we pray, we break out of the prison of blame and praise and enter into the houses of God's love. In this sense prayer is an act of martyrdom: in prayer we die to the self-destroying world of wounds and needs and enter into the healing light of Christ...

In a situation in which the world is threatened by annihilation, prayer does not mean much when we undertake it only as an attempt to influence God, or as a search for a spiritual fallout shelter, or as a source of consolation in stress-filled times. In the face of a nuclear holocaust prayer makes sense only when it is an act of stripping oneself of everything, even of our own lives, so as to be totally free to belong to God and God alone...

In the act of prayer, we undermine the illusion of control by divesting ourselves of all false belongings and by directing ourselves totally to the God who is the only one to whom we belong. Prayer, therefore, is the act of dying to all that we consider to be our own and of being born to a new existence which is not of this world.

Prayer is indeed a death to the world so that we can live for God.

The great mystery of prayer, however, is that even now it leads us already into God's house and thus offers us an anticipation of life in the divine Kingdom. Prayer lifts us up into the timeless immortal life of God.

There the meaning of the act of prayer in the midst of a world threatened by extinction becomes visible. By the act of prayer we do not first of all protest against those whose fears drive them to build nuclear warheads, missiles and submarines. By the act of prayer we do not primarily attempt to stop nuclear escalation and proliferation. By the act of prayer we do not even try to change people's minds and attitudes. All this is very important and much needed, but prayer is not primarily a way to get something done.

No, prayer is that act by which we appropriate the truth that we do not belong to this world with its warheads, missiles and submarines; we have already died to it so that not even a nuclear holocaust will be able to destroy us. Prayer is the act in which we willingly live through, in our own being, the ultimate consequences of nuclear destruction, and affirm in the midst of them that God is the God of the living and that no human power will ever be able to "unmake" God. In prayer we anticipate both our individual death and our collective death and proclaim that in God there is no death but only life. In prayer we undo the fear of death and therefore the basis of all human destruction.

Is this an escape? Are we running away from the very concrete issues that confront us? Are we "spiritualizing" the enormous problems facing us and thus betraying our time, so full of emergencies? This would be true if prayer became a way to avoid all concrete actions. But if prayer is a real act of death and rebirth, then it leads us right into the world where we must take action.

To the degree that we are dead to the world, we can live creatively in it. To the degree that we have divested ourselves of false belongings, we can live in the midst of turmoil and chaos. And to the degree that we are free of fear, we can move into the heart of danger.

Thus the act of prayer is the basis and source of all actions. When our actions against the arms race are not based on the act of prayer, they easily become fearful, fanatical, bitter, and more an expression of survival instincts than of our faith in God...

Entering the special solitude of prayer is a protest against a world of manipulation, competition, rivalry, suspicion, defensiveness, anger, hostility, mutual aggression, destruction and war. It is a witness to the all-empowering, all-healing power of God's love...

What do we do in our solitude? The first answer is nothing. Just be present to the One who wants your attention and listen! It is precisely in this "useless' presence to God that we can gradually die to our illusions of power and control and give ear to the voice of love hidden in the center of our being.

But "doing nothing, being useless," is not as passive as it sounds. In fact it requires effort and great attentiveness. It calls us to an active listening, in which we make ourselves available to God's healing presence and can be made new...

There are endless forms of prayer, both individual and communal, but if we truly want to die to the old war-making self and take up lodging in the house of peace, we must take a hidden meditative stand in the presence of God. This is truly the great spiritual challenge of the peacemaker.

— Peacework

THE STRANGER

Here Nouwen draws on his experience as part of the L'Arche community in Toronto, where he lived the last ten years of his life. In L'Arche communities handicapped adults live with able helpers. Nouwen was assigned to care for one of the most severely handicapped adults in the community, a young man named Adam. This experience gave him a new perspective on the gospel and the spiritual themes that run through all his books.

What is most striking about the resurrection stories is that the resurrection of Jesus is described as a hidden event. When we speak about the hidden life of Jesus we have to go far beyond his years at Nazareth. The great mystery of Jesus' life is that all of it has a hidden quality. First of all his conception and birth, then his many years lived in obedience to his parents, then his so-called public life in which he kept asking those he cured not to speak about their healing, then his death outside the walls of Jerusalem, between two criminals, and finally also his resurrection. Indeed, the resurrection of Jesus is not a glorious victory over his enemy. It is not a proof of his powers. It is not an argument against those who condemned him to death. Jesus did not appear to Annas, Caiaphas, Herod or Pilate, not even to his doubtful followers Nicodemus and Joseph of Arimathea. There is no gesture of "being right after all." There is no "I always told you so." There isn't even a smile of satisfaction.

No, the most decisive event in the history of creation is a deeply hidden event. Jesus appears as a stranger. Mary of Magdala sees a stranger in the garden. Cleopas and his friend find themselves walking with a stranger to Emmaus. The disciples see a stranger coming and think it is a ghost, and Peter, Thomas, Nathanael, John, James, and two other disciples hear a stranger calling out to them from the shore of the lake. How much of a stranger Jesus remains is succinctly expressed in that mysterious moment around the charcoal fire when Jesus offers bread and fish to his friend. John the Evangelist writes: "None of the disciples was bold enough to ask, 'Who are you?' They knew quite well it was the Lord" (John 21:12). Nowhere better than in this sentence is expressed the hiddenness of Jesus' resurrection. They knew who was giving them bread and fish, but didn't dare to ask who he was. The difference between knowing and not knowing, presence and absence, revealing and hiding, have been transcended in the presence of the risen Lord.

Here we touch the heart of L'Arche: revealing in hiddenness. I live at Daybreak with a profoundly handicapped twenty-five-year-old man called Adam. Adam does not speak; he cannot dress or undress himself; he cannot crawl, stand, or walk alone. He cannot eat without help, and suffers from seizures every day. But after living with him for eight months, carrying him to his bath, washing him, brushing his teeth, shaving his beard, combing his hair, and just sitting with him when he eats his breakfast, I am gradually discovering that he reveals his greatest gift to me in hiddenness.

People who visit us always ask: "Can Adam recognize you? Does he see you? Does he feel pain? Does he know the difference between good food and bad food?" These are the questions I asked when I first met Adam. But these are the curious questions about how normal he is, how much he is like me, how much he can be understood, how familiar he is. But now I am coming to sense that he reveals himself to me as a stranger, in hiddenness, and that there, in that unknown, unfamiliar, empty place, he holds the mystery of life for me.

It is hard to express myself well here. But what I want you to hear is that the hope that Adam offers is not bound to the places where he is like me, but held in a sacred hiddenness. The empty tomb is the first sign that something completely new has happened in the world. The longer I am with Adam, the less my hope is built in the possibility that one day he may smile, walk, or recognize my voice. If that were to happen I would be filled with joy, but I already know that it is his hiddenness that gives me life. Where he is most poor, there God dwells; where he is most silent, there God speaks; where he is most empty, there I find the signs of the resurrection. Adam is gradually explaining to me that meaning of the most used expression in liberation theology: "God's preferential option for the poor." Adam tells me that God dwells with the poor, not there where I can still connect my talents with what is left of theirs, but there where they are so completely empty that there is nothing for me to cling to and I am completely dependent on my faith.

"The Lord is risen, risen indeed." That is not a statement made by someone who finally had to give in to an argument. It is a statement of faith. When John entered the empty tomb and was faced with the linen cloths lying there, "he saw and he believed" (John 20:8). Seeing the poor like Adam and believing, that is the gift of L'Arche to the world.

What has the story of Adam to do with the big suffering of the world? It gives us a glimpse of the mystery that all suffering has a hidden quality, a quality of strangeness. Our temptation is to look at suffering as big, spectacular, noisy, and very imposing, the suffering that impatiently screams out: "What are you doing about it?" But in the center of all the hunger, homelessness, violence, torture, war, and the nuclear threat, there is a hidden anguish, a silent agony, an invisible loneliness, that nobody wants to touch. Jesus touched it, lived it, and carried it into the grave where he lifted it up to new life.

When we do not recognize the hidden quality of suffering we might easily be seduced into taking on the posture of problem-solvers who, in a great eagerness to help, add violence to violence. There is an enormously seductive quality to the big sufferings of the world. They can even have a great fascination for us. Countless generous people, wanting to be of service in the world, have been overpowered by the forces they tried to conquer. The anger, resentment, rivalry, and even revenge among many peace-people are a painful reminder of this.

The Adams among us, who live a silent anguish that we cannot reach with our need to help but only with our own inner poverty, keep revealing to us the suffering beyond all suffering. It is the voiceless suffering of a broken humanity that cannot be identified with any group, race, nationality, or culture. It is the suffering that is hidden not only in the heart of the poor and oppressed of Latin America, but also in the hearts of the wealthy businessman, the successful lawyer, and the famous movie star. It is the suffering that is hidden not only in the hearts of the malnourished children of the young towns at the outskirts of Lima, Peru, but also in the hearts of the lonely depressed students at Yale and Harvard...

Yes, it is that deeply hidden silent suffering that does not leave any human being untouched. Only by acknowledging this hidden suffering that binds our heart to the heart of all human beings can we become truly compassionate people who do not add violence to violence by good intentions, but who reverently bow before that sacred empty space where God chose to lay down his broken wounded body and from where he was raised up.

L'Arche is given to the world to remind us of the hidden quality of all suffering and to call us to live our small lives in compassionate solidarity with all humanity, a humanity destined to be raised up as a new creation.

I have an intuition that by reaching out to the suffering beyond all suffering we come in touch also with the source of joy, precisely because joy is not the opposite of suffering but hidden in the very center of it. Therefore, true joy is always found where we move to the very heart of the empty tomb of humanity.

— From "L'Arche and the World," *The Road to Peace*

SOURCES

Peacework: Prayer, Resistance, Community (Maryknoll, NY: Orbis Books, 2005).

The Road to Peace: Writings on Peace and Justice, ed. John Dear (Maryknoll, NY: Orbis Books, 1998).

The Selfless Way of Christ: Downward Mobility and the Spiritual Life (Maryknoll, NY: Orbis Books, 2007).

With Burning Hearts: A Meditation on the Eucharistic Life (Maryknoll, NY: Orbis Books, 1994; 2003).

T W E L V E

DOROTHY DAY

A New Kind of Holiness

Dorothy Day was born in Brooklyn in 1897. Though in her home God's name was never mentioned, she was attracted from an early age to the lives of the saints. She recalled being stirred by the stories of their charity toward the sick, the maimed, the leper. "But there was another question in my mind," she wrote. "Why was so much done in remedying the evil instead of avoiding it in the first place? ... Where were the saints to try to change the social order, not just to minister to the slaves, but to do away with slavery?" Over time such questions caused her to shun religion and to place her hopes instead in the progressive politics of the day. Her friends were Communists, socialists, and anarchists, with whom she worked on a variety of left-wing journals.

Despite the excitement of such activism, her early life was also marked by loneliness and a kind of moral and spiritual confusion. By her own account there was always a yearning for transcendence that distinguished her from her companions. As she herself later reflected (borrowing words from a character in Dostoevsky), "All my life I have been haunted by God."

This yearning ultimately brought her to the Catholic church. Despite her experience of sorrow and disappointment, in the end her conversion was not prompted by sadness but by an experience of "natural happiness," the experience of pregnancy and giving birth to a daughter. She felt such joy and an impulse of gratitude so large, as she called it, that it could be directed only to God. Yet her conversion was an enormous leap, beyond the comprehension of her common-law husband (as she called him). An agnostic and anarchist, he disdained Catholicism and warned that her embrace of religion would end their relationship. "It got to the

161

point," she wrote, "where it was the simple question of whether I chose God or man."

Compounding this anguish was her sense that the decision to become a Catholic also involved a betrayal of the working class. Though she believed the Catholic church was the church of the poor, it often seemed more like a friend of the rich, a protector of the status quo. She was at a loss about how to reconcile her nascent faith and her commitment to social justice.

Following her baptism in 1927 she spent five lonely years in the desert, praying that she might find a way of life "reconciling body and soul, this world and the next." Her search reached a crisis in December 1932 when she covered a "hunger march" of the unemployed in Washington, D.C., organized by her Communist friends. At the Shrine of the Immaculate Conception she prayed "that some way would open up for me to use what talents I possessed for my fellow workers, for the poor."

When she returned to New York she found waiting for her an unkempt older man with a thick French accent. He was Peter Maurin, a self-described "peasant-philosopher" who had determined that Day was the person to put his ideas into practice. He proposed a movement that would implement the social implications of the gospel. They would not wait for the church or state to enact such a program. They would begin to live today according to their vision of the future, working to create a society in which "it would be easier to be good."

From this encounter, and the Catholic Worker movement that ensued, Day found the work that engaged her for the rest of her life. The Catholic Worker *newspaper, first distributed on May 1, 1933, became the organ of a movement centered in "houses of hospitality" across the country. In these communities the traditional "works of mercy" (feeding the hungry, clothing the naked, sheltering the homeless) were joined with work for peace and social justice.*

So Day found an answer to her childhood question. Where were the saints to change the social order? It was a question to be answered with her own life. By serving Christ in the poor, while battling injustice, and trying through small means to create a peaceful alternative, she found the meaning of her vocation. She invented a new model of holiness.

The Catholic Worker was born in the midst of the Depression, and in its early years Day focused much attention on strikes, unions, and the rights of workers. The circulation of the paper swelled. But as her *pacifist position took hold, first in response to the Spanish Civil War, and then World War II, her voice was relegated more and more to the margins. Long before the phrase became common in the church, Day espoused a "seamless garment" approach to the defense of life. Her spirituality and her social witness were equally rooted in the radical implications of the Incarnation. In Christ God assumed our humanity. And we could not worship God without honoring God's image in our fellow human beings. We should feed them when they were hungry; shelter them when they were homeless. We should not torture them; we should not kill them.*

In the 1950s Day and the Catholic Worker took on a more activist profile. She was repeatedly jailed for refusing to take shelter during compulsory civil defense drills in New York City. In the 1960s her activities reflected the turbulence of the times — protesting the Vietnam War, fasting in Rome during the Second Vatican Council to advance the cause of peace. She was last arrested while picketing with the United Farm Workers in 1973 at the age of seventy-five.

By this time she was widely honored as the radical conscience of the American Catholic church. But her life was not primarily occupied by activism or protest. She was a woman of prayer, beginning each day with meditation on scripture, attending daily Mass, and reciting the breviary. By and large, her life was spent in very ordinary ways, her sanctity expressed not just in heroic deeds but in the mundane duties of everyday life. Her "spirituality" was rooted in a constant effort to be more charitable toward those closest at hand.

Day was particularly devoted to the "Little Flower," St. Therese of Lisieux, who taught the way of holiness that lies in all the small encounters and duties of our daily life, if performed in a spirit of love and attention to the presence of God. Dorothy Day embraced this teaching and drew out its social implications. She believed that each act of love, each work of mercy, might increase the balance of love in the world. Each act of protest or witness for peace — though apparently foolish and ineffective, no more than a pebble in a pond — might send forth ripples that could transform the world.

She died on November 29, 1980, at the age of eighty-three. Her cause for canonization was introduced in 2000, and so she was recognized by the title "Servant of God."

GLIMPSES OF GOD

This selection is taken from the introduction to Day's autobiographical book, From Union Square to Rome, *an early account of her conversion.*

It is difficult for me to dip back into the past, yet it is a job that must be done, and it hangs over my head like a cloud. St. Peter said that we must give a reason for the faith that is in us, and I am trying to give you those reasons...

While it is true that often horror for one's sins turns one to God, what I want to bring out in this book is a succession of events that led me to His feet, glimpses of Him that I received through many years which made me feel the vital need of Him and of religion. I will try to trace for you the steps by which I came to accept the faith that I believe was always in my heart. For this reason, most of the time I will speak of the good I encountered even amid surroundings and people who tried to reject God...

Much as we want to know ourselves, we do not really know ourselves. Do we really want to see ourselves as God sees us, or even as our fellow human beings see us? Could we bear it, weak as we are?...

I write in the very beginning of finding the Bible and the impression it made on me. I must have read it a good deal, for many passages remained with me through my earlier years to return and haunt me. Do you know the Psalms? They were what I read most when I was in jail in Occoquan [*for protests in favor of women's suffrage*]. I read with a sense of coming back to something that I had lost. There was an echoing in my heart. And how can anyone who has known human sorrow and human joy fail to respond to these words? "Out of the depths I have cried to thee, O Lord."

All through those weary first days in jail when I was in solitary confinement, the only thoughts that brought comfort to my soul were those lines in the Psalms that expressed the terror and misery of man suddenly stricken and abandoned. Solitude and hunger and weariness of spirit — these sharpened my perceptions so that I suffered not only my own sorrow but the sorrows of those about me. I was no longer myself. I was man. I was no longer a young girl, part of a radical movement seeking justice for those oppressed, I was the oppressed. I was that drug addict, screaming and tossing in her cell, beating her head against the wall. I was that shoplifter who for rebellion was sentenced to solitary. I was that woman who had killed her children, who had murdered her lover.

The blackness of hell was all about me. The sorrows of the world encompassed me. I was like one gone down into the pit. Hope had forsaken me. I was that mother whose child had been raped and slain. I was the mother who had borne the monster who had done it. I was even that monster, feeling in my own heart every abomination.

As I read this over, it seems, indeed, over-emotional and an exaggerated statement of the reactions of a young woman in jail. But if you live for long in the slums of cities, if you are in constant contact with sins and suffering, it is indeed rarely that so overwhelming a realization comes upon one. It often has seemed to me that most people instinctively protect themselves from being touched too closely by the suffering of others. They turn from it, and they make this a habit. The tabloids with their presentation of crime testify to the repulsive truth that there is a secret excitement and pleasure in reading of the sufferings of others. One might say there is a surface sensation in the realization of the tragedy in the lives of others. But one who has accepted hardship and poverty as the way in life in which to walk, lays himself open to this susceptibility to the sufferings of others.

And yet if it were not the Holy Spirit that comforted me, how could I have been comforted, how could I have endured, how could I have lived in hope?

The Imitation of Christ is a book that followed me through my days. Again and again I came across copies of it and the reading of it brought me comfort. I felt in the background of my life a waiting force that would lift me up eventually.

I later became acquainted with the poem of Francis Thompson, *The Hound of Heaven,* and was moved by its power. Eugene O'Neill recited it first to me in the back room of a saloon on Sixth Avenue where the Provincetown players and playwrights used to gather after the performances.

> I fled Him, down the nights and down the days;
> I fled Him, down the arches of the years;
> I fled Him, down the labyrinthine ways
> Of my own mind; and in the mist of tears
> I hid from Him.

Through all my daily life, in those I came in contact with, in the things I read and heard, I felt that sense of being followed, of being desired; a sense of hope and expectation.

Through those years I read all of Dostoevsky's novels and it was, as Berdyaev says, a profound spiritual experience. The scene in *Crime and Punishment* where the young prostitute reads from the New Testament to Raskolnikov, sensing the sin more profound than her own, which weighed upon him; that story, *The Honest Thief;* those passages in *The Brothers Karamazov;* the sayings of Father Zossima, Mitya's conversion in jail, the very legend of the Grand Inquisitor, all this helped to lead me on. The characters, Alyosha and the Idiot, testified to Christ in us. I was moved to the depths of my being by the reading of these books during my early twenties when I, too, was tasting the bitterness and the dregs of life and shuddered at its harshness and cruelty.

Do you remember that little story that Grushenka told in *The Brothers Karamazov?* "Once upon a time there was a peasant woman and a very wicked woman she was. And she died and did not leave a single good deed behind. The devils caught her and plunged her into a lake of fire. So her guardian angel stood and wondered what good deed of hers he could remember to tell God. 'She once pulled up an onion in her garden,' said he, 'and gave it to a beggar woman.' And God answered: 'You take that onion then, hold it out to her in the lake, and let her take hold and be pulled out. And if you pull her out of the lake, let her come to Paradise, but if the onion breaks, then the woman must stay where she is.' The angel ran to the woman and held out the onion to her. 'Come,' said he, 'catch hold, and I'll pull you out.' And he began cautiously pulling her out. He had just pulled her out, when the other sinners in the lake, seeing how she was being drawn out, began catching hold of her so as to be pulled out with her. But she was a very wicked woman and she began kicking them. 'I'm to be pulled out, not you. It's my onion, not yours.' As soon as she said that, the onion broke. And the woman fell into the lake and she is burning there to this day. So the angel wept and went away."

Sometimes in thinking and wondering at God's goodness to me, I have thought that it was because I gave away an onion. Because I sincerely loved His poor, He taught me to know Him. And when I think of the little I ever did, I am filled with hope and love for all those others devoted to the cause of social justice.

"What glorious hope!" Mauriac writes. "There are all those who will discover that their neighbor is Jesus himself, although they belong to the mass of those who do not know Christ or who have forgotten Him. And nevertheless they will find themselves well loved. It is impossible for any

one of those who has real charity in his heart not to serve Christ. Even
some of those who think they hate Him, have consecrated their lives
to Him; for Jesus is disguised and masked in the midst of men, hidden
among the poor, among the sick, among prisoners, among strangers.
Many who serve Him officially have never known who He was, and
many who do not even know His name, will hear on the last day the
words that open to them the gates of joy. "Those children were I, and I
those working men. I wept on the hospital bed. I was that murderer in
his cell whom you consoled."

But always the glimpses of God came most when I was alone. Objectors cannot say that it was fear of loneliness and solitude and pain
that made me turn to Him. It was in those few years when I was alone
and most happy that I found Him. I found Him at last through joy and
thanksgiving, not through sorrow.

Yet how can I say that either? Better let it be said that I found Him
through His poor, and in a moment of joy I turned to Him. I have said,
sometimes flippantly, that the mass of bourgeois smug Christians who
denied Christ in His poor made me turn to Communism, and that it was
the Communists and working with them that made me turn to God...

A mystic may be called a man in love with God. Not one who loves
God, but who is *in love with God.* And this mystical love, which is an
exalted emotion, leads one to love the things of Christ. His footsteps are
sacred. The steps of His passion and death are retraced down through the
ages. Almost every time you step into a Church you see people making
the Stations of the Cross. They meditate on the mysteries of His life,
death, and resurrection, and by this they are retracing with love those
early scenes and identifying themselves with the actors in those scenes.

When we suffer, we are told we suffer with Christ. We are "complet-
ing the sufferings of Christ." We suffer His loneliness and fear in the
garden when His friends slept. We are bowed down with Him under
the weight of not only our own sins but the sins of each other, of the
whole world. We are those who are sinned against and those who are
sinning. We are identified with Him, one with Him. We are members of
His Mystical Body.

Often there is a mystical element in the love of a radical worker for his
brother, for his fellow worker. It extends to the scene of his sufferings,
and those spots where he has suffered and died are hallowed. The names
of places like Everett, Ludlow, Bisbee, South Chicago, Imperial Valley,
Elaine, Arkansas, and all those other places where workers have suffered

and died for their cause have become sacred to the worker. You know this feeling as does every other radical in the country. Through ignorance, perhaps, you do not acknowledge Christ's name, yet, I believe you are trying to love Christ in His poor, in His persecuted ones. Whenever men have laid down their lives for their fellows, they are doing it in a measure for Him. This I still firmly believe, even though you and others may not realize it.

"Inasmuch as ye have done it unto one of the least of these brethren, you have done it unto me." Feeling this as strongly as I did, is it any wonder that I was led finally to the feet of Christ? . . .

It was from men such as these that I became convinced, little by little, of the necessity of religion and of God in my everyday life. I know now that the Catholic Church is the church of the poor, no matter what you say about the wealth of her priests and bishops. I have mentioned in these pages the few Catholics I met before my conversion, but daily I saw people coming from Mass. Never did I set foot in a Catholic church but that I saw people there at home with Him. First Fridays, novenas, and missions brought the masses thronging in and out of the Catholic churches. They were of all nationalities, of all classes, but most of all they were the poor. The very attacks made against the Church proved her Divinity to me. Nothing but a Divine institution could have survived the betrayal of Judas, the denial of Peter, the sins of many of those who professed her Faith, who were supposed to minister to her poor.

Christ is God or He is the world's greatest liar and imposter . . . And if Christ established His Church on earth with Peter as its rock, that faulty one who denied him three times, who fled from Him when he was in trouble, then I, too, wanted a share in that tender compassionate love that is so great. Christ can forgive all sins and yearn over us no matter how far we fall.

How I ramble on! I do it partly to avoid getting on to the work of this book. It will, no doubt, be disjointed, perhaps incoherent, but I have promised to write it. It entails suffering, as I told you, to write it. I have to dig into myself to get it out. I have to inflict wounds on myself. I have, perhaps, to say things that were better left unsaid.

After all, the experiences that I have had are more or less universal. Suffering, sadness, repentance, love, we all have known these. They are easiest to bear when one remembers their universality, when we remember that we are all members or potential members of the Mystical Body of Christ . . .

A conversion is a lonely experience. We do not know what is going on in the depths of the heart and soul of another. We scarcely know ourselves.   — *FUS*, 3–18

AIMS AND PURPOSES

An editorial published in the Catholic Worker

For the sake of new readers, for the sake of men on our breadlines, for the sake of the employed and unemployed, the organized and unorganized workers, and also for the sake of ourselves, we must reiterate again and again our aims and purposes.

Together with the Works of Mercy, feeding, clothing, and sheltering our brothers, we must indoctrinate. We must "give reason for the faith that is in us." Otherwise we are scattered members of the Body of Christ, we are not "all members one of another." Otherwise our religion is an opiate, for ourselves alone, for our comfort or for our individual safety or indifferent custom.

We cannot live alone. We cannot go to heaven alone. Otherwise, as Péguy said, God will say to us, "Where are the others?"

If we do not keep indoctrinating, we lose the vision. And if we lose the vision, we become merely philanthropists, doling out palliatives.

The vision is this. We are working for "a new heaven and new *earth,* wherein justice dwelleth." We are trying to say with action, "Thy will be done on *earth* as it is in heaven." We are working for a Christian social order.

We believe in the brotherhood of man and the Fatherhood of God. This teaching, the doctrine of the Mystical Body of Christ, involves today the issue of unions (where men call each other brothers); it involves Houses of Hospitality and farming communes. It is with all these means that we can live as though we believed indeed that we are all members one of another, knowing that when "the health of one member suffers, the health of the whole body is lowered." ...

We must practice the presence of God. He said that when two or three are gathered together, there He is in the midst of them. He is with us in our kitchens, at our tables, on our breadlines, with our visitors, on our farms. When we pray for our material needs, it brings us close to His humanity. He, too, needed food and shelter, He, too, warmed His hands at a fire and lay down in a boat to sleep.

When we have spiritual reading at meals, when we have the rosary at night, when we have study groups, forums, when we go out to distribute literature at meetings, or sell it on street corners, Christ is there with us. What we do is very little. But it is like the little boy with a few loaves and fishes. Christ took that little and increased it. He will do the rest. What we do is so little we may seem to be constantly failing. But so did He fail. He met with apparent failure on the Cross. But unless the seed fall into the earth and die, there is no harvest.

And why must we see results? Our work is to sow. Another generation will be reaping the harvest...

The work grows with each month, the circulation increases, letters come in from all over the world. It is a new way of life. But though we grow in numbers and reach far-off corners of the earth, essentially the work depends on each one of us, on our way of life, the little works we do.

"Where are the others?" God will say. Let us not deny Him in those about us. Even here, right now, we can have that new earth, wherein justice dwelleth!   —February 1940, *SW*, 91–92

ROOM FOR CHRIST

It is no use saying that we are born two thousand years too late to give room to Christ. Nor will those who live at the end of the world have been born too late. Christ is always with us, always asking for room in our hearts.

But now it is with the voice of our contemporaries that He speaks, with the eyes of store clerks, factory workers, and children that he gazes, with the hands of office workers, slum dwellers, and suburban house-wives that He gives. It is with the feet of soldiers and tramps that He walks, and with the heart of anyone in need that He longs for shelter. And giving shelter or food to anyone who asks for it, or needs it, is giving it to Christ.

We can do now what those who knew Him in the days of His flesh did. I am sure that the shepherds did not adore and then go away to leave Mary and her Child in the stable, but somehow found them room, even though what they had to offer might have been primitive enough. All that the friends of Christ did for Him in His lifetime, we can do. Peter's mother-in-law hastened to cook a meal for Him, and if anything in the Gospels can be inferred, it surely is that she gave the very best she had, with no thought of extravagance. Matthew made a feast for Him, inviting the whole town, so that the house was in an uproar of enjoyment, and the straitlaced Pharisees — the good people — were scandalized . . .

If we hadn't got Christ's own words for it, it would seem raving lunacy to believe that if I offer a bed and food and hospitality to some man or woman or child, I am replaying the part of Lazarus or Martha or Mary, and that my guest is Christ. There is nothing to show it, perhaps. There are no halos already glowing around their heads — at least ones that human eyes can see . . .

Some time ago I saw the death notice of a sergeant-pilot who had been killed on active service. After the usual information, a message was added which, I imagine, is likely to be imitated. It said that anyone who had ever known the dead boy would always be sure of a welcome at his parents' home. So, even now that the war is over, the father and mother will go on taking in strangers for the simple reason that they will be reminded of their dead son by the friends he made.

This is rather like the custom that existed among the first generations of Christians, when faith was a bright fire that warmed more than those who kept it burning. In every house then, a room was kept ready for any stranger who might ask for shelter; it was even called "the stranger's room"; and this not because these people, like the parents of the dead airman, thought they could trace something of someone they loved in the stranger who used it, not because the man or woman to whom they gave shelter reminded them of Christ, but because — plain and simple and stupendous fact — he *was* Christ.

It would be foolish to pretend that it is always easy to remember this. If everyone were holy and handsome, with "alter Christus" shining in neon lighting from them, it would be easy to see Christ in everyone. If Mary had appeared in Bethlehem clothed, as St. John says, with the sun, a crown of twelve stars on her head, and the moon under her feet, then people would have fought to make room for her. But that was not God's way for her, nor is it Christ's way for Himself, now when He is disguised under every type of humanity that treads the earth . . .

In Christ's human life, there were always a few who made up for the neglect of the crowd. The shepherds did it; their hurrying to the crib atoned for the people who would flee from Christ. The wise men did it, their journeys across the world made up for those who refused to stir one hand's breadth from the routine of their lives to go to Christ. Even the gifts the wise men brought have in themselves an obscure recompense and atonement for what would follow later in this Child's life. For they brought gold, the king's emblem, to make up for the crown of thorns that He would wear; they offered incense, the symbol of praise, to make up for the mockery and the spitting; they gave Him myrrh, to heal and soothe, and He was wounded from head to foot and no one bathed His wounds. The women at the foot of the Cross did it too, making up for the crowd who stood by and sneered.

We can do it too, exactly as they did. We are not born too late. We do it by seeing Christ and serving Christ in friends and strangers, in everyone we come in contact with.

All this can be proved, if proof is needed, by the doctrines of the Church. We can talk about Christ's Mystical Body, about the vine and branches, about the Communion of Saints. But Christ Himself has proved it for us, and no one has to go further than that. For He said that a glass of water given to a beggar was given to Him. He made heaven hinge on the way we act toward Him in His disguise of commonplace, frail, ordinary humanity.

Did you give Me food when I was hungry?

Did you give Me to drink when I was thirsty?

Did you give me clothes when My own were all rags?

Did you come to see Me when I was sick, or in prison or in trouble?

And to those who say, aghast, that they never had a chance to do such a thing, that they lived two thousand years too late, He will say again what they had the chance of knowing all their lives, that if these things were done for the very least of His brethren they were done to Him.

For a total Christian, the goad of duty is not needed — always prodding one to perform this or that good deed. It is not a duty to help Christ, it is a privilege. Is it likely that Martha and Mary sat back and considered that they had done all that was expected of them — is it likely that Peter's mother-in-law grudgingly served the chicken she had meant to keep till Sunday because she thought it was her "duty"? She did it gladly; she would have served ten chickens if she had had them.

If that is the way they gave hospitality to Christ, it is certain that that is the way it should still be given. Not for the sake of humanity. Not because it might be Christ who stays with us, comes to see us, takes up our time. Not because these people remind us of Christ, as those soldiers and airmen remind the parents of their son, but because they *are* Christ, asking us to find room for Him, exactly as He did at the first Christmas.

—December 1945, *SW*, 94–97

HERE AND NOW

We fill our days with activity, and when we start to think, to see how little we can do, when we contemplate the apparent hopelessness of the situation around us and our feeble attempts to love people and show our love by serving them, we are overcome by the seeming futility of it all. The others have the better part. They bring life forth. They bear children, and the teeming life about them carries with it to some extent its consolations together with its anguish. Father Damascus Winzen said at a retreat given at Maryfarm that one tragedy of today was a loss of the *joy of life*, joy in living, which men should have if they were healthy and happy. Children have it. You often see it in mothers, a placidity and serenity which is a quiet joy...

We want to be happy. We want others to be happy. We want to see some of this joy of life which children have, we want to see people intoxicated with God, or just filled with the good steady joy of knowing that Christ is King and that we are His flock and He has prepared for us a kingdom, and that God loves us as a father loves his children, as a bridegroom loves his bride, and that eye hath not seen nor ear heard what God hath prepared for us!...

We have not yet begun to know what men are capable of in the spiritual order. What growth, what joy!

Father Henri de Lubac, S.J., wrote recently, "It is not the proper duty of Christianity to form leaders — that is, builders of the temporal, although a legion of Christian leaders is infinitely desirable. Christianity must generate saints — that is, witnesses to the eternal. The efficacy of the saint is not that of the leader. The saint does not have to bring about great temporal achievements; he is one who succeeds in giving us at least a glimpse of eternity despite the thick opacity of time."

We are all called to be saints, St. Paul says, and we might as well get over our bourgeois fear of the name. We might also get used to recognizing the fact that there is some of the saint in all of us. Inasmuch as we are growing, putting off the old man and putting on Christ, there is some of the saint, the holy, the divine right here.

One of the features of the retreat at Maryfarm is the renewal of the baptismal vows. Most of us do not know that we have taken vows. One of the fellows said jovially, "Let me read them over to see if I want to renew them!" We have renounced the world, the flesh, and the devil, we have already done it, there is no help for it, we are Christians, we have put on Christ, there is the seed of divine life in us. But as to whether we remain idiots or morons or feebleminded in this life — this does not seem to occur to most of us. We have to grow, the egg has to hatch, it has to develop wings, else it becomes a rotten egg, as C. S. Lewis says. St. Augustine says that a mother delights in nursing her child, but she does not want it to remain a child always. She wants it to grow into a man.

We are called to be saints. Sometimes we don't see them around us, sometimes their sanctity is obscured by the human, but they are there nonetheless.

All this talk about saints, and our obligation to strive toward sanctity, is because there is a very subtle way of attacking the temporal aims of the Catholic Worker, our work in the fields of pacifism and Distributism, by saying, and in so saying dismissing us as quite beyond anyone's acceptance or imitation: "Oh, they are all saints down there at Mott Street!"

All the emphasis laid on our work for the poor, our breadline, our clothing line, our tenement-house shelter, our sharing with others, and with them the sights and sounds and smells of dirt and disease and destitution. Yet with all our sharing we hang on to too much. We have no right to talk of poverty in the face of the suffering in the world. Our farming communes are spoken of as utopian attempts to get families back on the land and to do away with the machine; we are looked upon as modern fathers of the desert who are fleeing the wrath to come. Our actions are admired and praised but only as palliatives and poultices, and our efforts to do away with the state by nonviolent resistance and achieving a distributist economy are derided and decried.

Of course we are few. But Marx and Engels and Trotsky and Stalin were few, but that did not keep them from holding *their* vision and studying and working toward it...

We believe that spiritual action is the hardest of all — to praise and worship God, to thank Him, to petition Him for our brothers, to repent our sins and those of others. This is action, just as the taking of cities is action, as revelation is action, as the Corporal Works of Mercy are action. And just to lie in the sun and let God work on you is to be sitting in the light of the Sun of Justice and the growth will be there, and joy will grow and spread from us to others. That is why I like to use so often that saying of St. Catherine of Siena, "All the Way to Heaven is Heaven, because He said I am the Way."   — 1949, *SW*, 100–104

INVENTORY

This last year at St. Joseph's House of Hospitality we gave out, roughly speaking and underestimating at that, 460,000 meals. Also 18,250 night's lodgings. That is what the world sees and if we wished to impress the world we would multiply this by eighteen years, and the figures would be truly impressive.

But suppose a mother should say in a plea for sympathy, "I've put one thousand and ninety-five meals on the table this last year. I've washed fifty thousand plates."

It is easy to see how foolish it is to look at things in this light, in this big way. I am sure that God is not counting the meals...

We all wish for recognition of one kind or another. But it is mass action people think of these days. They lose sight of the sacrament of the present moment — of the little way.

Like Lord Jim, in Conrad's story, we are all waiting for great opportunities to show heroism, letting countless opportunities go by to enlarge our hearts, increase our faith, and show our love for our fellows, and so for Him. As St. Paul says, it is by little and by little that we are saved — or that we fall. We are living in this world and must make choices now, choices which may mean the sacrifice of our lives, in the future, but for now our goods, our reputations even. Our work is called futile, our stand of little worth or significance, having no influence, winning no converts, ineffective if not a form of treason. Or it is termed defeatism, appeasement, escapism.

What a paradox it is, this natural life and this supernatural life. We must give up our lives to gain them, we must die to live, we must be pruned to bear fruit. Ah yes, when we are being called appeasers, defeatists, we are being deprived of our dearest goods — our reputation, honor, the esteem of men — and we are truly on the way to becoming the despised of the earth. We are beginning perhaps to be truly poor.

We are trying to spread the gospel of peace, to persuade others to extend the peace movement, to build up a mighty army of conscientious objectors. And in doing this we are accounted fools, and it is the folly of the Cross in the eyes of an unbelieving world.

Martyrdom is not gallantly standing before a firing squad. Usually it is the losing of a job because of not taking a loyalty oath, or buying a war bond, or paying a tax. Martyrdom is small, hidden, misunderstood. Or if it is a bloody martyrdom, it is the cry in the dark, the terror, the shame, the loneliness, nobody to hear, nobody to suffer with, let alone to save. Oh, the loneliness of all of us in these days, in all the great moments of our lives, this dying which we do, by little and by little, over a short space of time or over the years. One day is as a thousand in these crises. A week in jail is as a year.

But we repeat that we do see results from our personal experiences and we proclaim our faith. Christ has died for us. Adam and Eve fell, and Julian of Norwich wrote, the worst has already happened and been repaired. Christ continues to die in His martyrs all over the world, in His Mystical Body, and it is this dying, not the killing in wars, which will save the world.

Do we see results, do these methods succeed? Can we trust in them? Just as surely as we believe in "the little way" of St. Therese, we believe and know that this is the only success.   —January 1951, *SW,* 104–5

ON PILGRIMAGE

"Meditations for women," these notes should be called, jumping as I do from the profane to the sacred over and over. But then, living in the country, with little children, with growing things, one has the sacramental view of life. All things are His and all are holy.

I used to wish I could get away from my habit of constant, undisciplined reading, but in a family one is certainly cured of it. If you stop to read a paper, pick up a book, the children are into the tubs or the sewing machine drawers. Everything is interrupted, even prayers, since by nightfall one is too tired to pray with understanding. So I try to practice the presence of God after the manner of Blessed Lawrence, and pray without ceasing as St. Paul advised.   —*SW,* 211

◆ ◆ ◆

When you love people, you see all the good in them, all the Christ in them. God sees Christ, His Son, in us. And so we should see Christ in others, *and nothing else,* and love them. There can never be enough of it, there can never be enough thinking about it. St. John of the Cross said, that where there was no love, put love and you would draw love out. The principle certainly works. I've seen my friend Sister Peter Claver with that warm friendliness of hers which is partly natural, but is intensified and made enduring by grace, come into a place which is cold with tension and conflict, and warm the house with her love.

And this is not easy. Everyone will try to kill that love in you, even your nearest and dearest; at least, they will try to prune it. "Don't you know this, that, and the other things about this person? ... "

The antagonism often rises to a crescendo of vituperation, an intensification of opposition on all sides. You are quite borne down by it. And the only Christian answer is *love,* to the very end, to the laying down of your life.   —*SW,* 213–14

◆ ◆ ◆

Naturally speaking, people are filled with repulsion at the idea of holiness. We have so many sad examples of Pecksniffs in our midst. But we are filled with encouragement these days to find that it is not only the Catholic Workers but writers like Ignazio Silone, Aldous Huxley, and Arthur Koestler who are crying aloud for a synthesis — the saint-revolutionist who would impel others to holiness by his example...

Archbishop Robichaud, in his book *Holiness for All,* emphasizes the fact that the choice is not between good and evil for Christians — that it is not in this way that one proves one's love...

In all secular literature it has been so difficult to portray the good man, the saint, that Don Quixote is made a fool and Prince Myshkin an epileptic, in order to arouse the sympathy of the reader, appalled by unrelieved goodness. There are, of course, the lives of the saints, but they are too often written as though they were not in this world. We have seldom been given the saints as they really were, as they affected the lives of their times — unless it is in their own writings. But instead of that strong meat we are too generally given the pap of hagiography.

Too little has been stressed the idea that *all* are called. Too little attention has been placed on the idea of mass conversions. We have sinned against the virtue of hope. There have been in these days mass conversions to Nazism, Fascism, and Communism. Where are our saints to call the masses to God? Personalists first, we must put the question to ourselves. Communitarians, we will find Christ in our brothers and sisters.
                                                              —*SW,* 215–17

◆ ◆ ◆

"Hell is not to love anymore," writes Georges Bernanos in *The Diary of a Country Priest.* I felt when I read this that the blackness of hell must indeed have descended on Our Lord in His agony.

The one thing that makes our work easier most certainly is the love we bear for each other and for the people for whom we work. The work becomes difficult only when there is quarreling and dissension and when one's own heart is filled with a spirit of criticism.

In the past, when I have spoken on the necessity of mutual charity, of self-criticism rather than criticism of others, the accusation has been made that I talk to the men as though they were angels, that I do not see their faults. Which is certainly not true.

The difficulty for me is not in *not* seeing the other person's faults, but in seeing and developing his virtues...

Oh yes, my dear comrades and fellow workers, I see only too clearly how bad things are with us all, how bad you all are, and how bad a leader I am. I see it only too often and only too clearly. It is because I see it so clearly that I must lift up my head and keep in sight the aims we must always hold before us. I must see the large and generous picture of the new social order wherein justice dwelleth. I must hold always in mind the new earth where God's Will will be done as it is in heaven. I must hold it in mind for my own courage and for yours.

The new social order as it could be and would be if all men loved God and loved their brothers because they are all sons of God! A land of peace and tranquility and joy in work and activity. It is heaven indeed that we are contemplating...

Even the best of human love is filled with self-seeking. To work to increase our love for God and for our fellow man (and the two must go hand in hand), this is a lifetime job. We are never going to be finished.

Love and ever more love is the only solution to every problem that comes up. If we love each other enough, we will bear with each other's faults and burdens. If we love enough, we are going to light that fire in the hearts of others. And it is love that will burn out the sins and hatred that sadden us. It is love that will make us want to do great things for each other. No sacrifice and no suffering will then seem too much.

Yes, I see only too clearly how bad people are. I wish I did not see it so. It is my own sins that give me such clarity. If I did not bear the scars of so many sins to dim my sight and dull my capacity for love and joy, then I would see Christ more clearly in you all.

I cannot worry much about your sins and miseries when I have so many of my own. I can only love you all, poor fellow travelers, fellow sufferers. I do not want to add one least straw to the burden you already carry. My prayer from day to day is that God will so enlarge my heart that I will see you all, and live with you all, in His love.   —*SW,* 85–88

SOURCE

FUS   *From Union Square to Rome* (Maryknoll, NY: Orbis Books, 2006).

SW   *Dorothy Day: Selected Writings,* ed. Robert Ellsberg (Maryknoll, NY: Orbis Books, 1992).

Acknowledgments

While every effort has been made to identify and credit copyright holders, there may still be omissions and inadvertent errors. We will correct these in future printings of the volume. Further information on sources is indicated at the end of each chapter.

Thea Bowman
Sister Thea Bowman, *Shooting Star: Selected Speeches and Writings*, ed. Celestine Cepress, FSPA (Winona, MN: Saint Mary's Press, 1993). Excerpts reprinted by courtesy of Franciscan Sisters of Perpetual Adoration, Thea Bowman FSPA Collection, La Crosse, Wisconsin. Sr. Thea Bowman's address to the U.S. Bishops, "To Be Black and Catholic," *Origins* (July 6, 1989): 114–18. Used by permission of *Origins*, CNS – Catholic News Service, Washington, DC.

Catherine de Hueck Doherty
Selections from Catherine de Hueck Doherty, *Poustinia: Christian Spirituality of the East for Western Man* (Notre Dame, IN: Ave Maria Press, 1975); *Living the Gospel without Compromise* (Combermere, Ontario: Madonna House Publications, 2002); *The Gospel without Compromise* (Combermere, Ontario: Madonna House Publications, 1989); *Fragments of My Life* (Combermere, Ontario: Madonna House Publications, 1996), all reprinted with permission of Madonna House Publications (Combermere, Ontario).

Madeleine Delbrêl
Selections from Madeleine Delbrêl, *We, the Ordinary People of the Streets*, trans. David Louis Schindler, Jr. and Charles F. Mann (Grand Rapids, MI: William B. Eerdmans Publishing Company, 2000). Reprinted by permission of the publisher; all rights reserved.

Mohandas Gandhi
Writings of Gandhi copyright © Navajivan Trust, reprinted with permission of Navajivan Trust, Ahmedabad-380 014, Gujarat, India.

Thomas Merton
Thomas Merton, *Conjectures of a Guilty Bystander* (Garden City, NY: Doubleday, 1966). Copyright © 1966 by The Abbey of Gethsemani. Used by permission of Doubleday, a division of Random House.

Thomas Merton, *Honorable Reader: Reflections on My Work,* ed. Robert Daggy (New York: Crossroad, 1991). Used with permission of The Crossroad Publishing Company.

Henri Nouwen
Excerpts from *The Selfless Way of Christ: Downward Mobility and the Spiritual Life* (Maryknoll, NY: Orbis Books, 2007); *With Burning Hearts: A Meditation on the Eucharistic Life* (Maryknoll, NY: Orbis Books, 1994; 2003); *Peacework: Prayer, Resistance, Community* (Maryknoll, NY: Orbis Books, 2005); and *The Road to Peace: Writings on Peace and Justice,* ed. John Dear (Maryknoll, NY: Orbis Books, 1998) are reprinted by permission of the Henri Nouwen Legacy Trust *www.henrinouwen.org.*

Mother Teresa
Mother Teresa, *In the Heart of the World: Thoughts, Stories, and Prayers,* ed. Becky Benenate (Novato, CA: New World Library, 1997). Copyright © 1997 New World Library. Reprinted with permission of New World Library, Novato, CA. *www.newworldlibrary.com.*

Mother Teresa, *In My Own Words,* comp. José Luis González-Balado (Liguori, MO: Liguori Publications, 1996). Copyright © 1996. Used with permission of Liguori Publications, Liguori, MO 63057. 1-800-325-9521. *www.liguori.org.*

Excerpts from *The Mother Teresa Reader: A Life for God,* comp. LaVonne Neff (Ann Arbor, MI: Servant Publications, 1995); Mother Teresa, *Total Surrender,* ed. Brother Angelo Devananda (Ann Arbor, MI: Servant Books, 1985); Mother Teresa, *Jesus the Word to Be Spoken: Prayers and Meditations for Every Day of the Year,* comp. Brother Angelo Devananda (Ann Arbor, MI: Servant Books, 1986); *Mother Teresa, Heart of Joy: The Transforming Power of Self-Giving,* ed. José Luis González-Balado (Ann Arbor, MI: Servant Books, 1987); and Mother Teresa, *One Heart Full of Love,* ed. José Luis González-Balado (Ann Arbor, MI: Servant Books, 1984), all published by Servant Books. Used with permission of St. Anthony Messenger Press.

Mother Teresa of Calcutta, A Gift for God: Prayers and Meditations (New York: Harper & Row, 1975). Copyright © 1975 by Mother Teresa Missionaries of Charity. Reprinted by permission of HarperCollins Publishers.

Howard Thurman
Howard Thurman, *With Head and Heart: The Autobiography of Howard Thurman* (New York: Harcourt Brace and Co., 1979). Copyright © 1979 by Howard Thurman, reprinted by permission of Houghton Mifflin Harcourt Publishing Company.

Biographical prefaces have been adapted from Robert Ellsberg, *All Saints: Daily Reflections on Saints, Prophets, and Witnesses for Our Time* (New York: Crossroad, 1987) and *Blessed among All Women: Women Saints, Prophets, and Witnesses for Our Time* (New York: Crossroad, 2005); used with permission of The Crossroad Publishing Company.